SOLO COOKING

Mary Morris

Sampson Low

Acknowledgements
Cover photograph: Graham Bishop
Photography: Terry Pickering,
Colour Precision Studios, Chichester
Illustrations: Carol Swatton
Kitchen equipment and materials
for photography kindly supplied by
Snips of Chichester, Lavells,
Army & Navy Stores, Chichester
and *Macfarlanes*

Peacock Pie. The Literary
Trustees of Walter de la Mare
and The Society of Authors as
Their Representative.

The author would like to thank
Peter Robson for his assistance in
compiling articles in this book.

First published in 1980 by
Sampson Low, Berkshire House,
Queen Street, Maidenhead,
Berkshire SL6 1NF

SBN 562 00128 X

Designed and produced by Autumn Publishing Ltd,
10 Eastgate Square, Chichester, Sussex PO19 1JH
Filmset in 11/12 Bembo by Trident Graphics Limited,
Reigate, Surrey
Printed in Italy, by Poligrafici Calderara, Bologna.

CONTENTS

It's a very odd thing
As odd as can be
Whatever Miss T eats
Turns into Miss T

Walter de la Mare

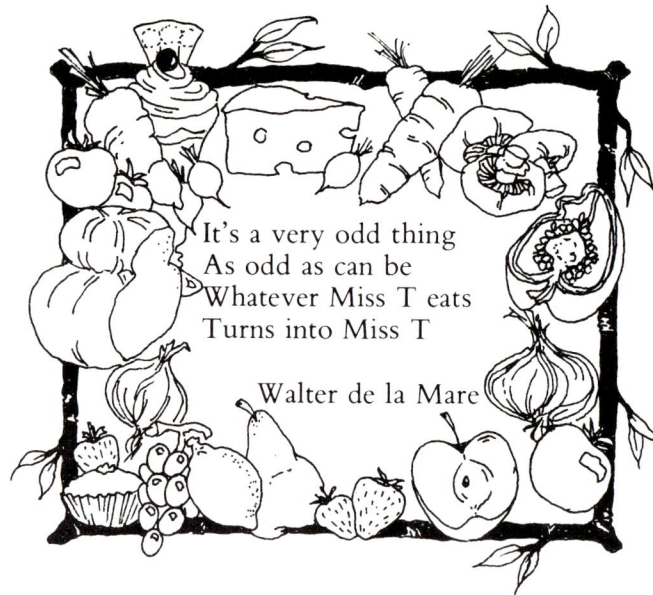

INTRODUCTION

This is not just another cookery book. It is called *Solo Cooking* because it has been written especially for those people who, at one time or another and for a variety of reasons, have to cook meals by themselves for themselves. How many of us just make ourselves a cup of tea or coffee and eat a few biscuits in place of light, but nutritionally balanced, lunch?

This book has been prepared for a special group of people – single people such as bachelors, students, those living away from home for the first time, widows and widowers, as well as busy housewives and wives who find themselves on their own when their husbands go away on business trips. The aim of this book is to inspire these people to cook themselves nourishing and appetizing meals.

Bearing in mind that cans of soup are often one of the quickest and easiest standbys for single people eating alone, I have included a number of recipes for home-made soup which are both satisfying and different. However, as these obviously take a bit longer to prepare than merely opening a can I have given quantities for two portions so that one portion can be served immediately, while the remainder can be chilled and served a couple of days later.

Many single people tend to disregard recipes calling for more unusual ingredients, such as half an avocado pear or two anchovy fillets, because they are impossible to purchase in 'solo' portions. To overcome this problem I have tried to include at least one other recipe to use up the remaining portion of that special ingredient, and to give a cross reference to the other recipe.

One question which I am frequently asked during my cookery lectures is: 'Can *anybody* become a good cook?' Well, I remember some years ago one excellent cook, whom I respected very much, remarked to me that 'to be a good cook, you have to be a little bit greedy'. That is very true, because almost every good cook appreciates good food – and I suppose most people can become greedy during their attempt to become a good cook!

More seriously, I think the only qualification needed to become a reasonably efficient cook is an interest in cooking. If the initial interest in cooking is developed and disciplined, then that cook can become an expert. If there is also talent and flair, then the cook can become an artist. Great cooks today are certainly regarded as artists – and are indeed rewarded as such! I hope you will discover that there is a lot of fun and enjoyment in cooking when you are cooking just for yourself – and when you are using this book.

One secret for success is to follow the recipes accurately. When preparing a recipe make sure you stick to one type of measure; in other words if you start using metric in a recipe, do not change to imperial or the USA measures (in brackets). Another is not to become too ambitious too soon. Otherwise you could find making a meal for yourself will become an extra chore – which is the last thing that should happen.

Finally, *please* do remember that after you have cooked a proper meal for yourself you need to enjoy eating it. This means sitting down comfortably at a table which has been properly set, or at the very least with a neatly laid tray. Arranging this only takes a moment and is well worthwhile.

UTENSILS

Chatting to a friend about how useful I thought my *Solo Cooking* book would be to young people leaving home for the first time, she suggested that I should perhaps include something about the very basic kitchen equipment every solo cook would need. It was a good suggestion. The only trouble is that the more one thinks about kitchen equipment, the more detailed any list becomes!

However, for a list of basic equipment, which would make anybody reasonably self-sufficient, I would suggest the following:

Several good sharp kitchen knives, preferably the carbon steel type, which are easier to sharpen than stainless steel; a wooden chopping board, which can double up as a bread board and even as a pastry board; a large frying-pan (skillet) and a small frying-pan (preferably with lids) which can be kept for quick meals, such as scrambled eggs at breakfast time or in the late evening.

After these, I think that every cook needs a roasting tin, bread knife, fish slice, potato peeler/corer, cheese grater, bottle opener, can opener, master key for cans of sardines and meats, spatula, kitchen scissors, metal colander, nylon sieve, and a large casserole with a well-fitting lid. A large and a small heavy-bottomed saucepan, a measuring jug, kitchen scales, measuring spoons, wire egg whisk, a couple of wooden spoons, a timer which can be wound up for several hours, a selection of ovenproof bowls – one of which should be shaped to be used also as a mixing bowl. Also, you should count among your basic kitchen equipment a kettle and half a dozen plastic boxes for storing food in the refrigerator. Among other essentials, I need hardly add a milk saucepan (with a lip), table knives, forks and spoons.

THE STORE CUPBOARD

Nobody can exist anywhere without provisions of some kind stored away, which is why a well-stocked and constantly replenished store cupboard can give you a sense of greater security.

Ideally, you should plan to keep in store those provisions which you know you will use on a day-to-day basis, as well as foods which can be used in emergencies, such as canned or dried vegetables. I suggest that anybody planning a store cupboard will find the following a useful check-list.

packet soups	canned tuna fish	sauces	spices
canned soups	canned sardines	canned rice pudding	salt, pepper, mustard
canned vegetables	drinking chocolate	pudding rice	plain flour (all purpose
canned meats	cocoa	long-grain rice	flour)
jellies	tea	semolina (flour)	self-raising flour (all
cake mixes	instant coffee	breakfast cereals	purpose flour with
scone mixes	Marmite	porridge oats	baking powder)
batter mixes	meat and chicken stock	instant mashed potatoes	sugar (brown, white and
custard powders	(bouillon) cubes	dried vegetables	castor)
instant desserts	jams	chutney (relish)	packet shredded suet
canned pilchards	marmalade	canned fruit	canned milk (evaporated
canned salmon	honey	herbs	and condensed)

There are some people who appear to have the happy knack of being able to make pots of soup from practically nothing. They probably won't stock up on packet and canned soups, but it really is important to tailor your store to suit yourself.

Solo Cooking takes this a step further, because, when you only use half a can or packet for one recipe I have provided another recipe which will use up what remains. For instance, the smallest size of something like tuna which is cheapest to buy is the 200 g/7 oz can. Yet a whole can of tuna is too rich for one person to consume in one meal. So after you have made your first tuna dish, I suggest the remainder might be used to make something like a Tuna and Noodle Casserole. This can be stored away in a freezer compartment. I have kept matters like this very much in mind, as you will see, throughout this book.

I think people who live alone or often cook for themselves do obviously enjoy variety in their meals, but they cannot afford to waste food. That is why in this book every time you open a perishable food for a recipe, I have suggested other appetizing ways of using anything left over.

It is important, of course, to keep your store cupboard as cool as possible and at a constant temperature. When I was a young girl I remember that in almost every house the larder was situated on the north side of the house. In my present home my larder faces south and I can well understand the wisdom behind that original thinking. I have grown an enormous bush against the outside wall of my larder to protect it from the sun and to help keep it as cool as possible.

Almost everything you place in your store cupboard or larder, will have a limited lifetime. So it is a good idea to label everything stored with the date of purchase. Apart from making sure that canned foods, which are more often than not kept for emergency meals, do not get pushed further and further to the back of the shelves until they are almost forgotten, it also ensures that you use your older stocks first.

Cans of jams, marmalades and honey, for example, should be used within three years from the date of purchase. Cans of fruit, milk and fish in tomato sauce, should all be eaten within twelve months.

Store cupboards should not only be well protected against flies and mice, but should also be well ventilated. A flow of air is essential to prevent the food from going bad. Ideally, you should always clean out your store cupboard once a month, making sure that the oldest purchases are moved to the front of the shelves and check, as far as possible, the condition of everything stored away.

Anything at all which appears contaminated or stale, or any cans which show the least signs of rust should be dealt with instantly: throw the stale or contaminated foods into the dustbin to prevent them affecting anything else.

11

VALUE-FOR-MONEY SHOPPING

Value for money is important to us all, especially to those elderly people and students, for instance, who live alone on fixed incomes or pensions and eat alone. I often suspect many of them do not nourish themselves as well as they should, because they believe it might be too expensive and too tedious to prepare a proper meal for themselves. This book, I hope, proves that this suspicion is wrong.

Some foods are always excellent value for money. Milk is the perfect food, because it can be used in so many different ways: as a drink, in puddings and sauces. It is probably the most important source of the vitamin riboflavin in most people's diets, which is why it should never be left for too long in sunlight or any strong light; otherwise it will lose its vitamin content.

Cheese is another wonderful value-for-money food. It keeps very well and can be used in many different ways for meals, so there is virtually no waste. It is also one of the cheapest sources of protein and is always readily available.

Meat is becoming more and more expensive these days. Fortunately, there are many cheaper cuts of meat and offal which are very good value for money, if they are properly prepared and cooked carefully and slowly. These include heart, liver, oxtail, kidney, shin of beef and neck of lamb, which can be just as appetizing and nourishing as the more expensive cuts.

Fish can be just as expensive as meat, but it is very nutritious and always tender. It is an excellent source of protein and is still a 'natural' food.

Always remember that value-for-money shopping means buying fruit and vegetables, as well as fish, when they are in season, when they are at their best and cheapest. When shopping for fish in season, the following table is a good reference:

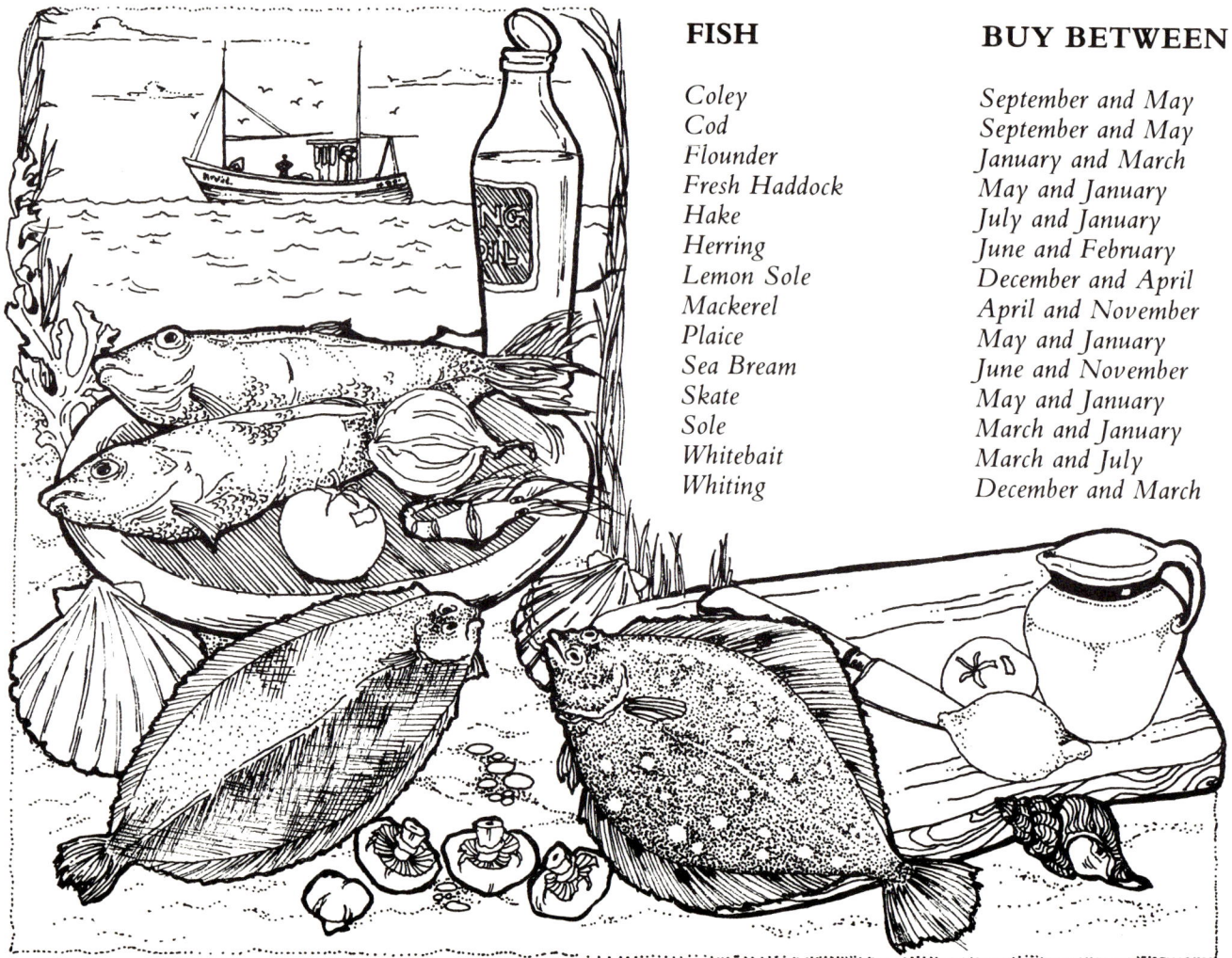

FISH	BUY BETWEEN
Coley	September and May
Cod	September and May
Flounder	January and March
Fresh Haddock	May and January
Hake	July and January
Herring	June and February
Lemon Sole	December and April
Mackerel	April and November
Plaice	May and January
Sea Bream	June and November
Skate	May and January
Sole	March and January
Whitebait	March and July
Whiting	December and March

Fish skin and bones can be boiled together for stock (bouillon), which can be used to make a delicious sauce to pour over your fish. So, even if you are buying a filleted fish, ask the fishmonger to wrap up some of the bones and skin to make your stock.

One problem which often crops up for the solo cook is buying in quantities small enough for just one person. It really can be difficult buying small amounts of anything you want. Yet, if we can buy just one lemon, why can't we, generally speaking, buy just one apple, or two tomatoes, or one small chop, or even two sausages, if that is all we require for ourselves?

I know there are some shopkeepers who do sell in small quantities to their regular customers, and they have nothing to lose by doing so, because the goodwill upon which their business depends starts with the customers.

Fuel economy is another way to make sure we get value for our money. Apart from buying our food, we also have to pay for the electricity or gas supplies which we use for cooking, so it pays to organize your cooking properly.

Obviously, the more you can cook on one hot-plate, gas-ring or in the oven at once, the better value you get from your fuel costs. There are many types of pots and pans with dividers in them which are ideal for this purpose. These will allow you to cook several foods at once; perhaps a meat dish in one section, vegetables in others and

possibly even a bowl containing a pudding in another!

Never use the oven for just one dish, but use the levels for cooking different things, some of which you can store or freeze for use later. That is why I have included in this book recipes for small cakes, which can be baked in the oven at the same time as a meat dish and a pudding.

Slow cookers are very good investments both for fuel economy and for cooking those cheaper cuts of meat to perfection. One beauty of them is that you can put everything into the cooker before going to work in the morning and return home to a perfectly cooked meal which has used very little fuel.

Pressure cookers can also be good investments for solo cooks, because they cook quickly, again saving on fuel costs. Foods like stews or casseroles, which are cooked in pressure cookers, are better when they are cooked in the evenings and re-heated the next day: this allows the full flavour of the food to develop. Single people will find pressure cookers a blessing, because vegetables, fruit, pudding and meat can be prepared quickly in the same cooker at the same time, without the risk of the cross-absorption of flavours.

Work out what you can afford to spend, then find the shops in your area which have reputations for providing the best possible quality at the most competitive prices. In this way, you can be certain of spending your money wisely.

HEALTHY EATING

Take almost any newspaper, magazine or cookery book and you will usually find something on the healthy approach to eating. A healthy diet is essential of course, and there is nothing very difficult about achieving it.

If possible, you should try to include the following in your diet each day: milk, some butter or margarine, together with a portion of meat, fish, eggs or cheese, in at least two of your meals. Add to each of those meals a generous helping of green vegetables, two slices of bread, some cereal and one piece of fresh fruit.

Fluids are also essential to a healthy diet, so you should drink about four glasses of water each day, which helps keep eyes bright and complexions clear.

A normal healthy diet must also include proteins, fats, carbohydrates, vitamins and minerals. Protein is provided by meat, fish, cheese, eggs, vegetables and nuts. There is no need to worry about buying steaks and other expensive foods to obtain protein; it is also available in cheaper meats such as liver, kidney and heart, as well as in chicken, fish, lentils, dried peas, beans and cheese, all of which can provide nourishing and economical meals.

Carbohydrates come from bread, potatoes, fruit, vegetables, oatmeal, sugar, syrups, flour, jams and dried fruits. Fats are obtained from eggs, milk, canned salmon, herrings, nuts, butter, margarine, bacon, lard, olive and other vegetable oils.

Generally, the salts needed in our daily diet are provided by the food we eat and from the salt used in food preparation and cooking. Iron, for example, is a mineral which we find particularly in liver, kidneys and corned beef. Calcium comes from dairy produce such as milk and cheese, and is also provided by green vegetables, sardines and canned salmon.

Vitamins are vital to good health, of course, but in fact we only require small, though regular, amounts and normally all our vitamin requirements can be obtained by following a well-balanced diet.

Vitamin A is most abundant in halibut liver oil and cod liver oil, but we can also get it from liver, dairy produce, eggs and vegetables. The vitamin B complex includes vitamin B1 and riboflavin, both of which are found in liver and wheatgerm. Riboflavin also comes from milk and eggs, while vitamin B1 can be found in beans, peas, peanuts, oatmeal and bacon.

Nicotinic acid is also an important member of the vitamin B complex and it is derived from meat extracts such as Bovril, brewers' yeast and Marmite, and from liver, kidneys, wheatgerm, fish and meat.

The richest sources of vitamin C are rose-hips, which are used to make a syrup, blackcurrants, and citrus fruits such as oranges, lemons and grapefruit. This vitamin is also present in fresh vegetables and fresh fruit generally.

Although vitamin D is found in foods such as sardines, herrings, canned salmon, cod liver oil and margarine, it can also be absorbed into your body in a most surprising way: by sun-bathing!

Finally, there are two other vitamins – E, which comes from milk and wheatgerm, and K which can be found in green peas and cabbage.

Whenever I discuss nutrition, many people often raise the topic of so-called health foods! Some years ago, health food 'addicts' were regarded as cranks, but today opinion is swinging the other way, because there are so many people who claim that they would never dream of picking up a can opener, or opening a packet of convenience food. If you enjoy organically-grown 'health' or 'whole' foods and can afford them, then by all means do so. However, if you buy fresh products in season from your butcher, greengrocer and fishmonger, you are buying the most natural of all foods at the best prices.

Cream of Cheese Soup

INGREDIENTS *(2 servings)*

1 medium potato
1 small onion – finely chopped
300 ml/½ pint (1¼ cups) chicken stock (chicken broth)
150 ml/¼ pint (⅔ cup) milk
50 g/2 oz (4 tablespoons) Cheddar cheese – grated
salt and freshly ground black pepper
1 tomato – skinned, de-seeded and diced

METHOD

Cooking time: 15 minutes

1   Peel the potato and cut into small dice.

2   Put the potato, onion and stock (broth) into a saucepan and bring to the boil. Reduce the heat and simmer until the vegetables are tender. Remove from the heat.

3   Stir in the milk, cheese and tomato. Season to taste.

4   Re-heat thoroughly, but do not allow the soup to boil, as this would toughen the cheese.

Serve very hot. Garlic bread is good with this soup.

German Kidney Soup

Follow this soup with a little fresh fruit for a perfect light lunch.

INGREDIENTS *(2 servings)*

100 g/4 oz (¼ lb) ox kidney
15 g/½ oz (2 teaspoons) butter
½ a small onion – finely chopped
1×15 ml spoon/1 tablespoon (1 tablespoon) chopped fresh herbs (parsley and marjoram) OR a large pinch of dried herbs
2×5 ml spoons/2 teaspoons (2 teaspoons) plain flour (all purpose flour)
600 ml/1 pint (2½ cups) hot beef stock (beef broth)
1×15 ml spoon/1 tablespoon (1 tablespoon) milk
1 egg yolk
salt and freshly ground black pepper

To garnish:
fried croûtons
chopped parsley

METHOD

Cooking time: 25 minutes

1   Soak the kidney in salted water for 10 minutes. Rinse, remove the core and cut into bite size pieces.

2   Heat the butter, add the onion and cook until golden.

3   Add the kidney and herbs and cook gently for a few minutes. Stir in the flour and cook for 2 minutes.

4   Gradually add the hot stock (broth), stirring constantly. Allow to simmer until the kidney is tender.

5   Pour the milk into the egg yolk and beat together. Stir in a ladleful of hot stock (broth). Pour the mixture back into the soup and heat gently until the soup thickens. Do not allow to boil.

Serve very hot, sprinkled with parsley and accompanied by croûtons.

Chilled Avocado Cream Soup

Rub the cut side of the other half with lemon juice, cover with cling film and use for Baked Avocado, page 58.

INGREDIENTS

½ large avocado
15 g/½ oz (1 tablespoon) butter
1 shallot OR slice of onion – finely chopped
150 ml/¼ pint (⅔ cup) chicken stock (chicken broth)
3×15 ml spoons/3 tablespoons (3 tablespoons) single cream (coffee cream)
lemon juice
salt and freshly ground black pepper

To garnish:
spring onion (scallion) – finely chopped

Chilled Avocado Cream Soup

METHOD

Cooking time: 10 minutes

1. Melt the butter in a small pan, stir in the shallot (or onion slice) and cook gently until soft.

2. Add the stock (broth) and bring to the boil. Remove from the heat.

3. Stone, peel and slice the avocado into the liquidizer, add the stock (broth), switch on to high speed until smooth.

4. Pour into a bowl, cool slightly, stir in the cream and lemon juice. Season and chill.

Serve very cold, sprinkled with the chopped spring onion (scallion).

Onion and Tomato Bisque

INGREDIENTS *(2 servings)*

2 rashers streaky bacon – de-rinded and chopped
15 g/½ oz (1 tablespoon) butter
225 g/8 oz (½ lb) onions – peeled and finely sliced
1 large potato – peeled and sliced
300 ml/½ pint (1¼ cups) stock (broth)
1×225 g/8 oz (½ lb) canned tomatoes
pinch of grated nutmeg
salt and freshly ground black pepper
2×15 ml spoons/2 tablespoons (2 tablespoons) sour
cream

To garnish:
fried bread croûtons

METHOD

Cooking time: about 45 minutes

1   Melt the butter and fry the bacon until crisp. Remove the bacon, add the onions and potatoes and cook for 5 minutes. Stir in the stock (broth), tomatoes and their juice, nutmeg, half the bacon and seasoning. Cover the pan and simmer until tender.

2   Pour the soup into a liquidizer and blend at high speed or rub through a sieve.

3   Re-heat the soup; serve hot with a spoonful of cream in each bowl. Sprinkle with the remaining bacon.

Olive Chowder

INGREDIENTS *(2 servings)*

50 g/2 oz (4 tablespoons) stuffed olives – drained and finely chopped
½ clove garlic – crushed
150 ml/¼ pint (⅔ cup) chicken stock (chicken broth)
1 egg yolk – beaten
120 ml/4 fl oz (½ cup) double cream (heavy cream)
salt and freshly ground black pepper

METHOD

Cooking time: 20 minutes

1   Put the olives, garlic and stock (broth) in a pan and simmer for 15 minutes. Remove from heat.

2   Stir the well-beaten egg yolk into the cream and pour into the soup. Re-heat very carefully until soup thickens slightly, but do not boil.

Hot Cucumber Soup

INGREDIENTS *(2 servings)*

2×15 ml spoons/2 tablespoons (2 tablespoons) spring onions (scallions) – finely sliced
15 g/½ oz (1 tablespoon) butter
350 ml/12 fl oz (1½ cups) chicken stock (chicken broth)
2×5 ml spoons/2 teaspoons (2 teaspoons) fresh dill – chopped OR 1×2.5 ml spoon/½ teaspoon (½ teaspoon) dried dill
½ large cucumber – peeled, halved, de-seeded and finely diced
salt and freshly ground black pepper

To garnish:
few browned flaked almonds

METHOD

Cooking time: 15 minutes

1   Melt the butter in a small pan, add the spring onions (scallions) and sauté gently until soft.

2   Pour in the chicken stock (chicken broth) and dill, bring to the boil and simmer for 5 minutes.

3   Stir in the cucumber and allow to simmer for a further 3 minutes. Serve very hot garnished with the almonds.

This can also be a summer time soup. Allow it to cool a little, stir in 2×15 ml spoons/2 tablespoons (2 tablespoons) of double cream (heavy cream). Chill and sprinkle with browned flaked almonds.

Sweetcorn Cream Soup

Sweetcorn Cream Soup

INGREDIENTS *(2 servings)*

15 g/½ oz (1 tablespoon) butter
15 g/½ oz (1 tablespoon) plain flour (all purpose flour)
120 ml/4 fl oz (½ cup) chicken stock (chicken broth)
200 g/7 oz (⅔ cup) canned sweetcorn
Salt and freshly ground black pepper
dash of Worcestershire sauce
4×15 ml/4 tablespoons (¼ cup) double cream (heavy cream) OR *evaporated milk*

To garnish:
1 slice bacon
chopped parsley

METHOD

Cooking time: 20 minutes

1 Melt butter in a saucepan. Stir in the flour and cook for a few minutes.

2 Remove from the heat and gradually stir in the stock (broth), seasoning and Worcestershire sauce. Bring gently to the boil and remove from the heat.

3 Open the can of corn, strain off the liquid and stir the corn into the pan. Bring back to the boil and simmer gently for 8 minutes.

4 Meanwhile, fry bacon until crisp. Stir the cream into the soup. Serve with the bacon crumbled on top and garnish with chopped parsley.

Calcutta Egg

Another variation on a theme. If you like a hot
curry flavour, add a little more paste to the
sausage meat. Try finely chopped peanuts in place
of the breadcrumbs once in a while.

INGREDIENTS

75 g/3 oz (6 tablespoons) pork sausage meat
salt and freshly ground black pepper
1×5 ml spoon/1 teaspoon (1 teaspoon) curry paste
1 egg – hard-boiled
*1×5 ml spoon/1 teaspoon (1 teaspoon) plain flour (all
purpose flour)*
1 small egg – beaten
25 g/1 oz (2 tablespoons) soft white breadcrumbs
oil or fat for deep frying

To garnish:
sprig of parsley

METHOD

Cooking time: 15 minutes

1 Work together the sausage meat, curry paste
   and seasoning until well mixed.

2 Roll the egg in the flour and mould the
   sausage meat around it.

3 Dip this mixture into the beaten egg and then
   in the breadcrumbs, pressing them well.

4 Heat the oil to 190°C 375°F Gas mark 5 and
   cook the egg until golden brown. Drain on
   kitchen paper and serve hot or cold with sweet
   chutney (relish).

Garnish with parsley.

Calcutta Egg is delicious served with a simple salad.

Croque Monsieur

This is a delicious and satisfying snack, but if you have a hearty appetite double the quantities to make 4 sandwiches. Both cheeses are suitable but Gruyère gives the essential 'gooeyness' and authentic flavour.

INGREDIENTS

2 thin slices of bread – crusts removed
50 g/2 oz (4 tablespoons) Gruyère or Cheddar cheese – grated
1×15 ml spoon/1 tablespoon (1 tablespoon) single cream (light cream)
1×5 ml spoon/1 teaspoon (1 teaspoon) Dijon mustard
1 thin slice of ham
1 egg – beaten
25 g/1 oz (2 tablespoons) butter

Croque Monsieur.

METHOD

Cooking time: 10 minutes

1 Mix the cheese with the cream and spread each slice with it.

2 Place the ham on one slice, spread with mustard and top with the remaining slice of bread, cheese side down. Press well together.

3 Pour the beaten egg on to a plate, dip the sandwich in and make sure it is completely covered.

4 Melt the butter. When it is foaming, fry the sandwich until it is golden brown on both sides.

Serve hot, with extra mustard and a tomato salad.

Low Calorie Stuffed Tomato

Low Calorie Stuffed Tomato

If you are not concerned with calorie intake, substitute cream cheese for the cottage cheese, and mayonnaise for the salad cream and it then becomes a 'spoil yourself' special.

INGREDIENTS

1 large firm tomato
1 small egg – hard-boiled
25 g/1 oz (2 tablespoons) cottage cheese
2×5 ml spoons/2 teaspoons (2 teaspoons) low calorie salad cream
1 thin spring onion (scallion) – finely sliced
salt and freshly ground black pepper

To garnish:
2 small lettuce leaves
1 black olive or black grape

METHOD

1 Cut a slice from the top of the tomato and put aside.

2 Scoop out the centre and seeds of the tomato into a small bowl.

3 Shell and chop the egg.

4 Add the cottage cheese to the bowl and beat well with the tomato pulp until smooth.

5 Stir in the salad cream, chopped egg, spring onion (scallion) and seasoning.

6 Arrange the lettuce leaves on a small dish. Pile the mixture into the tomato shell and place on the dish. Garnish with olive or grape. Chill before serving.

Chicken Liver Scramble

INGREDIENTS

25 g/1 oz (2 tablespoons) butter
2 chicken livers – trimmed and diced
1×15 ml spoon/1 tablespoon (1 tablespoon) soft white breadcrumbs
1 tomato – skinned, de-seeded and diced
salt and freshly ground black pepper
1 egg – beaten
1 slice of hot toast

METHOD

Cooking time: 8 minutes

1 Mix together the breadcrumbs, liver, tomato and beaten egg. Season well.

2 Melt the butter in a small pan. When foaming pour in the mixture and cook over gentle heat until the egg thickens.

Serve immediately on hot toast garnished with a sliced black olive.

Cheese Pudding

INGREDIENTS

1 egg
50 g/2 oz (4 tablespoons) mature Cheddar cheese – grated
1×5 ml spoon /1 teaspoon (1 teaspoon) made mustard
salt and freshly ground black pepper
150 ml/¼ pint (⅔ cup) milk
15 g/½ oz (1 tablespoon) soft white breadcrumbs

METHOD

Cooking time: 15–20 minutes
Oven: 190°C 375°F Gas mark 5

1 Beat the egg lightly and add the cheese, mustard and seasoning.

2 Bring the milk to the boil, pour over the egg mixture and stir in the crumbs.

3 Lightly grease a small pie dish and turn the pudding into it. Bake in the centre of a pre-heated oven for 15 minutes, or until set, puffed and golden brown.

Serve immediately with a green salad.

Toledo Toast

INGREDIENTS

1 large onion – sliced
25 g/1 oz (2 tablespoons) butter
salt and freshly ground black pepper
1 round of hot buttered toast
2 thin slices Cheddar cheese
English mustard

METHOD

Cooking time: 10 minutes

1 Melt the butter and cook the sliced onion carefully until a deep golden brown. Spread over the toast and season.

2 Spread the cheese slices with mustard and lay, mustard side down, over the onions.

3 Place under a hot grill (broiler) until the cheese melts.

Serve very hot, garnished with sliced olive.

Glamorgan Sausages

Here is a regional recipe from Wales which deserves to be better known. It makes much out of little but be sure to use a well flavoured Cheddar cheese. The crumbs reserved for coating could be replaced by ground almonds – particularly useful for vegetarians.

INGREDIENTS

75 g/3 oz (6 tablespoons) soft white breadcrumbs
40 g/1½ oz (3 tablespoons) Cheddar cheese – grated
1×5 ml spoon/1 teaspoon (1 teaspoon) onion – finely chopped
pinch of mixed herbs
pinch of dry mustard
salt and freshly ground black pepper
1 small egg – separated
a little oil or fat for shallow frying

METHOD

Cooking time: 10 minutes

1   Take 25 g/1 oz (2 tablespoons) of the breadcrumbs and reserve.

2   Mix together the remaining breadcrumbs and dry ingredients with the yolk of egg.

3   Roll into sausage shapes on a floured board.

4   Lightly beat the egg white. Dip the sausages into it, then roll in the reserved breadcrumbs, pressing them on.

5   Heat a little oil or cooking fat in a shallow pan and fry gently until golden. Eat hot or cold, garnished with a sprig of parsley.

Serve with tomato sauce.

Glamorgan Sausages

Sardine and Egg Savoury

INGREDIENTS

1 large egg – hard-boiled
1 tin sardines – drained
salt and freshly ground black pepper
15 g/½ oz (1 tablespoon) butter
25 g/1 oz (2 tablespoons) soft white breadcrumbs
4×15 ml spoons/4 tablespoons (¼ cup) milk

METHOD

Cooking time: 15 minutes
Oven: 190°C 375°F Gas mark 5

1 Shell and chop the egg, then skin and bone the sardines and mash. Mix together the egg and fish and season well.

2 Melt the butter, add the breadcrumbs, milk and egg-fish mixture. Pour into a small greased ovenproof dish, flake a little butter over the top and bake in a pre-heated oven for 15 minutes, *or* cook under the grill (broiler) if you prefer.

Serve hot, garnished with celery, accompanied by hot toast and fresh tomato salad.

Lunchtime Crumpets

INGREDIENTS

2 crumpets
25 g/1 oz (2 tablespoons) butter
1 small tomato – skinned
50 g/2 oz (4 tablespoons) trimmings of cooked ham or chicken
2 thin slices Cheddar cheese

METHOD

1 Toast the crumpets and butter them, using half the total quantity. Keep hot.

2 Slice the tomato. Chop the meat very finely. Mix with the remaining butter and season well.

3 Divide the tomato slices between the crumpets, spread the meat mixture over, and lay the cheese slices on top.

4 Grill (broil) until bubbling.

Savoury Cheese Spread

INGREDIENTS

225 g/8 oz (½ lb) well flavoured Cheddar cheese – grated
1 small carrot – grated
1 small onion – grated
small bunch of mustard and cress – chopped
salt and freshly ground black pepper
2 eggs
1×15 ml spoon/1 tablespoon (1 tablespoon) milk
15 g/½ oz (1 tablespoon) butter

METHOD

1 Mix together the cheese, carrot, onion and cress, and season whilst the butter is melting in a small pan.

2 Beat the eggs lightly, add the milk and scramble them in the hot butter. Remove from the heat and stir in the cheese mixture, mixing well until the cheese is melted. (A few drops of Worcestershire sauce may be added if liked).

3 Pour into an earthenware or glass dish. When completely cold cover with lid or cling film.

Tomatoes Nice Style with sautéed mushrooms.

Tomatoes Nice Style

When you are entertaining these make a good starter; serve one to each person, but as a main course for yourself, have two.

INGREDIENTS

2 large firm tomatoes
salt and freshly ground black pepper
2×5 ml spoons /2 teaspoons (2 teaspoons) fresh parsley
– chopped
½ clove of garlic
2 eggs
1×5 ml spoon/1 teaspoon (1 teaspoon) butter
25 g/1 oz (2 tablespoons) Cheddar cheese – grated

METHOD

Cooking time: 20 minutes
Oven: 180°C 350°F Gas mark 4

1   Cut the top off each tomato, remove a little of the flesh, season the insides and put a piece of garlic into each. Place in a buttered baking dish and bake in a pre-heated oven for 6 minutes.

2   Remove from the oven and take out the garlic pieces. Sprinkle the insides with the parsley and break an egg carefully into each. Flake the butter over and return to the oven for 10 minutes, or until the egg is just set.

3   Sprinkle with the cheese and brown slightly under the grill (broiler).

Madras Onion

Spanish onions are larger and milder than either French or English and are particularly suited to stuffing. Leftover cold meat mixed with a little gravy is an alternative to the curried chicken.

INGREDIENTS

1 large onion
salt and freshly ground black pepper
1×15 ml spoon/1 tablespoon (1 tablespoon) cooking oil
1×225 g/8 oz (8 oz) can curried chicken
squeeze of lemon juice
25 g/1 oz (2 tablespoons) soft white breadcrumbs
15 g/½ oz (1 tablespoon) butter

To garnish:
2×5 ml spoons/2 teaspoons (2 teaspoons) Mango chutney
sprig of watercress

METHOD

Cooking time: 30 minutes

1 Peel the onion carefully, keeping the root end intact. Place in a saucepan of cold water, add a little salt, cover and bring to the boil and simmer for 15 minutes.

2 Drain the onion well, allow to cool until you can handle it. Cut it in half and remove the centre part of each. Keep the shells warm.

3 Chop the centre part, heat the oil in a saucepan and add the onion; cook gently until soft. Stir in the curried chicken, lemon juice and 1×15 ml spoon/1 tablespoon (1 tablespoon) of the crumbs.

4 Arrange the onion shells in an ovenproof dish and fill the centres with the chicken mixture. Sprinkle the tops with the remaining crumbs. Flake the butter over and place under a pre-heated grill until golden. Garnish with the chutney and watercress.

Baked Tomato Pudding

INGREDIENTS

250 g/8 oz (½ lb) tomatoes
100 g/4 oz (¼ lb) breadcrumbs
1 small onion – finely chopped
salt and freshly ground black pepper
2×5 ml spoons/2 teaspoons (2 teaspoons) parsley – chopped
1×2.5 ml spoon/½ teaspoon (½ teaspoon) Marmite or yeast extract – dissolved in a little hot water
2 small eggs
1 slice of streaky bacon – finely chopped
50 g/2 oz (4 tablespoons) Cheddar cheese – grated

To garnish:
2 grilled bacon rolls

METHOD

Cooking time: 30 minutes
Oven: 180°C 350°F Gas mark 4

1 Peel the tomatoes, chop coarsely and add to the breadcrumbs, onion, parsley, bacon and cheese.

2 Beat the eggs and add the dissolved Marmite.

3 Combine the two mixtures and season to taste. Pour into a greased ovenproof dish and bake in a pre-heated oven for 25 minutes until puffed and golden. Garnish with the bacon rolls.

Anchovy Toastie

The Danish open sandwich is famous. Usually thought of in terms of the cold table, this is a hot one. Vary the savoury meringue by substituting the cheese for finely chopped ham or spring onion. Use the remaining anchovies for Salade Niçoise, page 37.

INGREDIENTS

1 circle of bread cut from a thick slice
1 egg – separated
1×5 ml spoon/1 teaspoon (1 teaspoon) Parmesan or Cheddar cheese – grated
2 anchovy fillets – split in half

Anchovy Toastie is a quick, satisfying snack.

METHOD

Cooking time: 10 minutes

1 Lightly toast one side of the bread.

2 Whisk the egg white with a tiny pinch of salt until stiff. Fold in the cheese.

3 Spread the egg and cheese meringue over the untoasted side of the bread, leaving a depression in the centre. Grill until lightly coloured.

4 Drop the raw yolk into the centre and arrange a lattice of anchovy over the top.

5 Toast lightly until egg sets.

Spicy Cheese Bites

Make a batch of these, frying as many as you need, and freezing the remainder until required. If you are entertaining serve them with drinks in place of a starter.

INGREDIENTS

100 g/4 oz (8 tablespoons) Cheddar cheese – grated
2×15 ml spoons/2 tablespoons (2 tablespoons) plain flour (all purpose flour)
1×2.5 ml spoon/½ teaspoon (½ teaspoon) salt
1×2.5 ml spoon/½ teaspoon (½ teaspoon) chilli powder
pinch of marjoram
1 egg white
3×15 ml spoons/3 tablespoons (3 tablespoons) chopped walnuts
a little oil for frying

METHOD

Cooking time: 10 minutes

1 In a large bowl, mix together the cheese, flour, salt, chilli powder and marjoram.

2 Whip the egg white until stiff and combine with the dry ingredients. Form into balls and roll in the walnuts. Chill well.

3 Heat the oil and sauté the balls until golden. Drain on kitchen paper. Serve hot, sprinkled with parsley.

Cheese and Almond Meringues

When separating eggs for meringues, take great care to keep the white completely clear of any trace of yolk. The whisk and bowl should be scalded and dried to remove all traces of grease as it affects the whipping properties of the white.

INGREDIENTS

2 egg whites
salt and cayenne pepper
6 almonds – finely chopped
1×5 ml spoon/1 teaspoon (1 teaspoon) parsley – finely chopped
1×15 ml spoon/1 tablespoon (1 tablespoon) Parmesan cheese – grated
oil for deep frying

METHOD

Cooking time: 5 minutes

1 While the oil is heating, put the egg whites into a large bowl and add a few grains of salt. Whisk until very stiff but not dry, and then carefully fold in the remaining ingredients.

2 Drop 1×15 ml spoon/1 tablespoon (1 tablespoon) of the meringue into the hot oil and cook until golden. Drain well on kitchen paper.

Serve very hot, garnished with tomato and watercress. Try a little tartare sauce with them.

Cream Cheese Pâté

INGREDIENTS

15 g/½ oz (1 tablespoon) butter
1 small onion – very finely sliced
75 g/3 oz (6 tablespoons) cream cheese
½ clove garlic – crushed
6 black olives – stoned (pitted) and finely chopped
50 g/2 oz (4 tablespoons) peeled prawns (shrimp)
salt and freshly ground black pepper
squeeze of lemon juice

METHOD

Cooking time: 5 minutes

1 Melt the butter, add the onion, cook very gently until lightly coloured.

2 Put the cream cheese into a bowl and beat in the onion, followed by remaining ingredients. It should be well seasoned.

Pack into a small pot, cover and refrigerate for up to a week. Serve with hot toast.

Danish Open Sandwiches

Creating toppings for Danish open sandwiches is half the fun of making them. Two or three of them constitute a perfect light meal when the ingredients are carefully balanced. Here are a few ideas for you to try – the possibilities are endless. Use white, wholemeal or, preferably, rye bread.

ROAST BEEF

Slice of buttered bread, completely covered with slice of cold roast beef. Garnish with a spoonful of horseradish sauce, pickled onions, stuffed olives and a sprig of parsley.

HAM

Slice of buttered bread, covered with a lettuce leaf, and then a slice of cooked ham. Garnish with apple sauce, stoned (pitted) prunes, and 2 apple slices.

VEGETARIAN

Slice of bread spread with crunchy peanut butter. Garnish with grated raw carrot, potato salad, black olives and sprigs of parsley.

SHRIMP

Slice of buttered bread, covered with slices of hard-boiled egg and peeled shrimps. Garnish with mayonnaise, lemon and cucumber twists.

CHICKEN

Slice of buttered bread, covered with shredded lettuce leaf, cold cooked sliced chicken, and 2 slices of crispy fried and crumbled bacon. Garnish with mayonnaise, and fresh orange twist.

CHEESE

Slice of buttered bread, covered with cream cheese, rings of sweet red pepper, black grapes and watercress.

Tempt yourself with these tasty Danish Open Sandwiches.

Mayonnaise

Do not try to make mayonnaise with cold eggs and oil. They must be at room temperature. Carefully remove every trace of white from the yolks. In my experience there is no finer mayonnaise than that made by hand with olive oil. If it curdle's put another egg yolk in a separate bowl and gradually add the mayonnaise.

INGREDIENTS

2 egg yolks
1×5 ml spoon/1 teaspoon (1 teaspoon) Dijon mustard
salt, white pepper and cayenne pepper to taste
2×15 ml spoons/2 tablespoons (2 tablespoons) white wine vinegar
few drops lemon juice
300 ml/½ pint (1¼ cups) best olive oil

METHOD

1 Place the yolks in a bowl. Blend in the mustard, salt, white pepper and a few grains of cayenne pepper. Beat well with a wooden spoon. This is an important point – if they are not worked well at this stage they will not absorb the large quantity of oil, and may curdle.

2 Beat a few drops of oil into the mixture, then continue whisking in the oil, a small amount at a time, until a thick emulsion forms. Thin it down with a little vinegar. Carry on with the oil and vinegar until all the oil has been absorbed. The amount of vinegar is rather a matter of taste. The final result should be a very thick shiny sauce. Finish with a few drops of lemon juice. Adjust the seasoning. Store the mayonnaise in a sterilized airtight jar in a cool place. It will keep almost indefinitely.

The colour and flavour may be varied with different additions such as crushed garlic, finely chopped fresh herbs, tomato purée or curry paste.

Pauline's Curried Salmon

This may seem an odd mixture – I first tried it in Barbados, with trepidation, but found it delicious – nothing ventured, nothing gained!

INGREDIENTS

15 g/½ oz (1 tablespoon) butter
1 small onion – peeled and finely chopped
2×5 ml spoons/2 teaspoons (2 teaspoons) curry powder
2×5 ml spoons/2 teaspoons (2 teaspoons) plain flour (all purpose flour)
150 ml/¼ pint (⅔ cup) chicken stock (chicken broth)
1×5 ml spoon/1 teaspoon (1 teaspoon) lemon juice
2×5 ml spoons/2 teaspoons (2 teaspoons) sweet chutney (relish)
1×175 g/6 oz (6 oz) can of salmon

METHOD

Cooking time: 35 minutes

1 Melt the butter, add the onion and cook for 2 minutes. Stir in the curry powder, cook for 3 minutes, then add the flour and continue cooking for another 2 minutes. Remove from the heat, pour the stock (broth) in gradually, bring to the boil, reduce heat and add lemon juice and chutney (relish). Allow to simmer for 15 minutes.

2 Add the contents of the tin of salmon to the curry sauce. Heat thoroughly, but do not allow to boil or break up the fish.

Serve on a hot dish garnished with lemon and parsley. Buttered noodles with this dish make a change from boiled rice.

Shrimp and Egg Aspic

Shrimp and Egg Aspic

INGREDIENTS

150 ml/¼ pint (⅔ cup) aspic jelly (packet)
50 g/2 oz (4 tablespoons) peeled prawns (shrimp)
1 egg – hard-boiled and chopped
½ small red or green pepper – de-seeded and finely chopped
1×15 ml spoon/1 tablespoon (1 tablespoon) thick mayonnaise
salt and freshly ground black pepper
½ cucumber

To garnish:
cucumber slices
orange segments

METHOD

1   Make up the aspic jelly and allow to cool.

2   Pour a little into a small mould and place in refrigerator to set.

3   Chop the prawns (shrimp), and the egg and pepper and bind with mayonnaise. Stir in 1×15 ml spoon/1 tablespoon (1 tablespoon) of the cool, but still liquid, aspic.

4   Cut diamond shaped pieces of cucumber and dip them in the aspic. Arrange them in a pattern in the centre of the mould. Chill again.

5   Pour a little more of the aspic into the mould and when set fill with the prawn mixture to within 2 cm/¾ inch of the top of the mould.

6   Top up the mould with liquid aspic and leave to set.

Decorate a plate with the garnish. Dip the mould in hot water for a few seconds then turn onto the plate. Using the same quantity of aspic, any small amounts of fish, poultry, meat or vegetables can be made up in this way.

Shrimp and Egg Platter

Shrimp and Egg Platter

INGREDIENTS

*50 g/2 oz (4 tablespoons) peeled prawns (shrimp) –
fresh or frozen*
*2×15 ml spoons/2 tablespoons (2 tablespoons)
mayonnaise*
salt and freshly ground black pepper
pinch of dry mustard
*1×2.5 ml spoon/½ teaspoon (½ teaspoon) Worcestershire
sauce*
1 hard-boiled egg
3 spring onions (scallions) – finely sliced
washed and dried lettuce leaves
paprika pepper

To garnish:
4 tomato wedges
cress

METHOD

1 If using frozen prawns (shrimp) – defrost. Put
the prawns (shrimp) in a bowl, and add the
mayonnaise, mustard, Worcestershire sauce,
seasoning and spring onions (scallions).

2 Arrange the lettuce leaves on a plate and top
with the prawn (shrimp) mixture. Peel the egg
and cut into quarters. Place around the dish.
Sprinkle with paprika.

Garnish with tomato and cress.

Salade Niçoise

INGREDIENTS

a few crisp lettuce leaves
1 egg – hard-boiled
1 tomato – skinned and sliced
1 potato – cooked, cooled and cubed
2×15 ml spoons/2 tablespoons (2 tablespoons) green beans – cooked and cooled (optional)
1×200 g/7 oz (7 oz) can of tuna fish
1×50 g/2 oz (2 oz) can of anchovy fillets
a few black olives
1×15 ml spoon/1 tablespoon (1 tablespoon) French dressing (Italian dressing)
½ clove of garlic – crushed

To garnish:
chopped parsley

METHOD

1 Rinse the lettuce leaves and shake dry. Tear into pieces and place in shallow bowl.

2 Peel the egg, cut into quarters and add to the bowl, together with the potato, beans and tomato.

3 Remove the tuna from the can and reserve half. Break the other half into bite size pieces and add to the salad.

4 Remove the anchovies from the can and reserve all except four. Arrange these in a lattice over the salad with the olives.

5 Mix the garlic with French dressing (Italian dressing) and pour over the salad just before serving. Garnish with chopped parsley.

The remaining tuna can be made into Tuna and Noodle Casserole, page 60. The remaining anchovies can be used for Anchovy Toastie, page 29.

Salade Niçoise, a delicious and satisfying salad dish.

Fruit and Fish Salad

Fruit and fish are a good combination. This makes a delicious summer meal. Vary the fruit according to availability or use canned fruit.

INGREDIENTS

175 g/6 oz white fish fillet (cod, haddock, plaice, sole, etc.) cooked, flaked and chilled
½ stalk of celery – finely chopped
1 dessert apple – peeled, cored and sliced
3 or 4 black or green grapes – pipped and halved
15 g/½ oz (1 tablespoon) flaked almonds
2×15 ml spoons/2 tablespoons (2 tablespoons) double cream (heavy cream) – whipped
1×15 ml spoon/1 tablespoon (1 tablespoon) sweet pickle (relish)
1×15 ml spoon/1 tablespoon (1 tablespoon) salad cream (mayonnaise)
salt and freshly ground black pepper
washed and dried lettuce leaves

To garnish:
spring onion (scallion) 'brushes'
orange segments
olives

METHOD

1   Combine the fish, celery, fruit and almonds in a bowl.

2   Fold the pickle (relish) and salad cream (mayonnaise) into the whipped cream.

3   Gently mix the cream mixture into the fish and fruit. Chill.

Serve on the lettuce leaves, garnished with spring onions (scallions), orange segments and olives.

Fruit and Fish Salad

38

Simon's Spare Ribs

These ribs are sold for Chinese cooking, not to be confused with the pork joint, also called spare ribs.

INGREDIENTS

500 g/1 lb (1 lb) meaty pork spare ribs – cut into pieces
4×15 ml spoons/4 tablespoons (¼ cup) dry or medium sherry
2×15 ml spoons/2 tablespoons (2 tablespoons) red wine vinegar
2×15 ml spoons/2 tablespoons (2 tablespoons) soft brown sugar (light brown sugar)
2×15 ml spoons/2 tablespoons (2 tablespoons) soy sauce

To garnish:
fresh tomato wedges

METHOD

Cooking time: 1–1½ hours
Oven: 180°C 350°F Gas mark 4

1   Arrange the spare ribs in a single layer in a large shallow baking dish.

2   Mix the remaining ingredients together and pour over the ribs. Bake in a pre-heated oven, turning and basting frequently. When the ribs are ready the fat will have cooked out of them and they will be glazed, tender and delicious. Garnish with tomato wedges.

Serve with a baked jacket potato and hot apple sauce. (A small can of apple sauce is an ideal portion for one and can be easily heated up).

Apple Temptation

INGREDIENTS

50 g/2 oz (4 tablespoons) sausage meat
2×5 ml spoons/2 teaspoons (2 teaspoons) onion – very finely chopped
1 slice of streaky bacon – chopped
pinch of mixed herbs
2×5 ml spoons/2 teaspoons (2 teaspoons) butter
salt and freshly ground black pepper
1 large cooking apple
2×15 ml spoons/2 tablespoons (2 tablespoons) beef or chicken stock (broth)
1 slice of fried bread

To garnish:
few sprigs of watercress

METHOD

Cooking time: about 45 minutes
Oven: 190°C 375°F Gas mark 5

1   Mix together the sausage meat, onion, bacon and herbs.

2   Melt the butter and cook the mixture gently until the onion is soft.

3   Wash and core the apple, scooping out enough flesh to allow for the stuffing. Nick the skin around the middle.

4   Chop the apple pulp and mix into the sausage stuffing and season well.

5   Place the apple in a greased ovenproof dish and pour in the stock (broth). Fill the centre with the stuffing.

6   Bake in a pre-heated oven for about 45 minutes or until tender.

Serve the apple on fried bread and pour the pan juices over. Garnish with watercress.

Gammon Steak Tivoli

INGREDIENTS

1 gammon steak
15 g/½ oz (1 tablespoon) butter – melted
2 mushrooms (optional)
2 tomatoes
salt and freshly ground black pepper

For the Sauce:
15 g/½ oz (1 tablespoon) butter
15 g/½ oz (1 tablespoon) onion – finely chopped
15 g/½ oz (1 tablespoon) plain flour (all purpose flour)
150 ml/¼ pint (⅔ cup) milk
40 g/¼ pint (3 tablespoons) Danish Blue (semi-hard, mould-ripened) cheese

To garnish:
a few chopped walnuts
sprig of watercress

Serve Gammon Steak Tivoli with crispy potato croquettes and buttered spinach.

METHOD

1 Remove the rind from the gammon and snip the fat at regular intervals to prevent curling.

2 Place on grill (broiler) rack and brush with melted butter. Cut the tomatoes in half, slice the mushrooms in the grill (broiler) pan, brush with butter and season with salt and pepper. Replace the rack and cook the bacon under a moderate heat until tender and slightly browned. Remove to a hot plate and keep warm. Continue cooking the tomatoes and mushrooms if necessary, then remove them to the hot dish. Reserve the juices in the pan.

3 *Make the sauce:* Melt the butter in a small saucepan. Add the onion and cook gently until soft. Stir in the flour and cook for 3 minutes. Gradually add the milk and the juices from the pan, stirring continuously and cook until the sauce is thick and smooth. Crumble the cheese and stir in over a very low heat until it melts. Pour over the gammon and garnish with the walnuts and watercress.

Red Flannel Hash

Red Flannel Hash

This dish is delicious served with onion rings dipped in milk, dusted with flour and fried until they are golden brown.

INGREDIENTS

1 small pickled beetroot – chopped
1 medium potato – boiled and chopped
3 slices of corned beef – chopped
salt and freshly ground black pepper
hot water
1×15 ml spoon/1 tablespoon (1 tablespoon) good dripping or oil
1×15 ml spoon/1 tablespoon (1 tablespoon) cream

METHOD

Cooking time: 15 minutes

1 Mix together the beetroot, potato and corned beef in a bowl. Season well.

2 Heat the dripping or oil in a heavy frying pan, add the mixture and moisten with a little hot water. Cover and cook slowly until golden and crisp underneath.

3 Pour the cream over the top and brown under a pre-heated grill (broiler). Garnish with the onion rings and parsley.

Boeuf Bourguignonne

This is a French classic – to spoil yourself one evening. Good quality meat is essential.

INGREDIENTS

25 g/1 oz (2 tablespoons) butter
25 g/1 oz (2 tablespoons) seasoned plain flour (all purpose flour)
175 g/6 oz (6 oz) rump steak – cubed
100 g/4 oz (¼ lb) small button onions – peeled
50 g/2 oz (½ cup) button mushrooms
1 clove of garlic – crushed
salt and freshly ground black pepper
150 ml/¼ pint (⅔ cup) beef stock (beef broth)
150 ml/¼ pint (⅔ cup) burgundy OR any dry red wine
1×5 ml spoon/1 teaspoon (1 teaspoon) tomato purée

METHOD

Cooking time: 20 minutes

1   Melt the butter, toss the meat into the seasoned flour and colour quickly in the butter. Add the onions and colour lightly, then add the mushrooms and garlic.

2   Pour in the stock (broth), wine and purée. Season lightly. Bring to the boil, reduce heat immediately and simmer for 20 minutes until tender.

Serve garnished with parsley and croûtons. Don't forget your glass of burgundy to go with it!

Spaghetti Alla Carbonara

INGREDIENTS

1 egg
1 small clove garlic – crushed
2×15 ml spoons/2 tablespoons (2 tablespoons) grated Parmesan or Cheddar cheese
1×15 ml spoon/1 tablespoon (1 tablespoon) milk
salt and freshly ground black pepper
2 slices of bacon
2×5 ml spoons/2 teaspoons (2 teaspoons) oil
100 g/4 oz (¼ lb) spaghetti – cooked and drained

METHOD

Cooking time: 15 minutes

1   Beat the egg and milk together, add the cheese and season.

2   Heat the oil, fry the bacon until crisp, remove, crumble and return to the pan with the garlic. Pour over the spaghetti and toss well.

3   Add the egg mixture; heat through carefully, tossing well together.

Serve very hot, sprinkled with walnuts and cheese.

Steak De Courcy

INGREDIENTS

50 g/2 oz (4 tablespoons) Stilton cheese – crumbled
2×5 ml spoons/2 teaspoons (2 teaspoons) olive oil
½ clove garlic – crushed
1×15 ml spoon/ 1 tablespoon (1 tablespoon) brandy
salt and freshly ground black pepper
1×75 g/6 oz (6 oz) fillet steak

METHOD

Cooking time: about 10 minutes

1   Brush both sides of the steak with a little oil.

2   Mash together the cheese, remaining oil, garlic and brandy.

3   Grill the steak to your liking and remove it to a hot ovenproof dish.

4   Spread the cheese mixture over the top and place under a pre-heated grill (broiler) until the cheese bubbles.

Bitkis à la Russe

Do not be tempted to leave out the bread and water treatment in this recipe. It alters the texture of the meat mixture, making it light and crumbly. Choose these when you are entertaining; they can be made the night before, will wait in a low oven indefinitely and are economical.

INGREDIENTS

100 g/4 oz (¼ lb) minced beef (ground beef)
1 small onion
a little parsley – chopped
1 slice crustless white bread soaked in cold water
salt and freshly ground black pepper
½ clove garlic – crushed (optional)
oil for frying
2×15 ml spoons/2 tablespoons (2 tablespoons) yoghurt
175 ml/6 fl oz (⅔ cup) condensed tomato soup
a few black olives (optional)

To garnish:
sprig of parsley

METHOD

Cooking time: 45 minutes
Oven: 190°C 375°F Gas mark 5

1   Place the meat in a bowl. Very finely chop the onion and add to the meat with the chopped parsley and plenty of seasoning.

2   Squeeze the bread as dry as possible and work it into the meat mixture, adding 1×15 ml spoon/1 tablespoon (1 tablespoon) of the cold water. On a wet surface, shape the mixture into 2 cakes.

3   Heat a little oil in a pan and fry the meat until brown on both sides, then place in an ovenproof dish.

4   Add the garlic (if used) to the tomato soup and pour over the cakes. Then bake in a pre-heated oven for about 15 minutes.

5   Remove from the oven, add the olives and the yoghurt and return to the oven for another 10 minutes.

Serve garnished with parsley.

Somerset Lambs' Tongues

A small can of skinned lambs' tongues can be used in many ways other than cold with salad.

INGREDIENTS

150 ml/¼ pint (⅔ cup) cider
1 clove
25 g/1 oz (2 tablespoons) sultanas
15 g/½ oz (1 tablespoon) soft brown sugar (light brown sugar)
1×5 ml spoon/1 teaspoon (1 teaspoon) cornflour (corn starch)
few flakes of butter
squeeze of lemon juice
1×175 g/6 oz (6 oz) can lambs' tongues

To garnish:
2 slices of apple

METHOD

Cooking time: 10 minutes

1   Put the cider, clove and sultanas in a small pan, bring to the boil and simmer for 5 minutes. Remove the clove.

2   Slake the cornflour (corn starch) with a little cider or water, add the sugar and pour into the hot cider. Bring to the boil, stirring continually until the sauce thickens. Whisk in the butter and lemon juice.

3   Slice the tongues and put them into the sauce. Heat carefully – do not allow to boil.

Serve on a hot dish garnished with apple slices. Potato croquettes make a good accompaniment.

Marmalade Porkers

Marmalade Porkers

INGREDIENTS

1 medium potato – peeled and sliced
4×15 ml spoons/4 tablespoons (¼ cup) water
2×15 ml spoons/2 tablespoons (2 tablespoons) white wine (optional)
2 pork sausages
1 dessert apple – cored and cut into rings
salt and freshly ground black pepper
4×15 ml spoons/4 tablespoons (¼ cup) orange marmalade

METHOD

Cooking time: 25 minutes

1   Put the water, wine and potato slices into a pan, add a little salt, bring to the boil, reduce the heat, cover and simmer until tender – about 10 minutes. Remove to a warm dish and keep hot.

2   In the same pan, cook the sausages slowly until the fat runs, then add the apple rings and cook, turning to brown evenly. Remove to a hot serving plate.

3   Add the marmalade to the pan, cook and stir until melted. Gently mix in the potato, heating carefully. Season to taste.

4   Garnish with parsley or watercress.

Danish Olives

INGREDIENTS

2 slices of bacon
a little fat for frying
15 g/½ oz (1 tablespoon) butter
½ onion – very finely chopped
25 g/1 oz (2 tablespoons) fresh breadcrumbs
2×5 ml spoons/2 teaspoons (2 teaspoons) parsley – finely chopped
little grated lemon rind
salt and freshly ground black pepper
50 g/2 oz (4 tablespoons) long grain rice – freshly boiled and hot

For the sauce:
15 g/½ oz (1 tablespoon) butter
15 g/½ oz (1 tablespoon) plain flour (all purpose flour)
150 ml/¼ pint (⅔ cup) chicken stock (broth)
grated rind and juice of half a small lemon

METHOD

Cooking time: 40 minutes

1   Trim the rind from the slices of bacon.

2   *Make the stuffing:* melt the butter, add the onion and cook gently. Stir in the breadcrumbs, parsley and lemon rind. Season.

3   Spread the stuffing on the bacon slices and roll up. Tie with fine string.

4   Melt a little fat and cook the bacon rolls until golden, then reduce the heat to a minimum and leave to cook for another 10 minutes. Meanwhile, boil and drain the rice. Keep bacon and rice hot.

5   *Make the sauce:* melt the butter, add the flour and cook for 1 minute. Gradually pour in the stock (broth), stirring well, and bring to the boil, add lemon juice and rind. Cook for 3 minutes.

6   Spread the cooked rice on a hot serving dish. Place the 'olives' on top. Pour over the sauce and garnish with chopped walnuts.

Danish Olives served with a tangy lemon sauce.

Hawaiian Pork Patties

INGREDIENTS

100 g/4 oz (¼ lb) pork sausage meat
2×15 ml spoons/2 tablespoons (2 tablespoons) soft
white breadcrumbs
2×5 ml spoons/2 teaspoons (2 teaspoons) fresh herbs –
finely chopped (include sage or mint if possible)
salt and freshly ground black pepper
1×15 ml spoon/1 tablespoon (1 tablespoon) plain flour
(all purpose flour)
1 egg – beaten
2×15 ml spoons/2 tablespoons (2 tablespoons) dried
breadcrumbs
deep or shallow fat for frying
2 slices of tinned pineapple
French mustard
sugar

Hawaiian Pork Patties with pineapple rings.

METHOD

Cooking time: 20 minutes

1 Work the sausage meat, soft breadcrumbs, herbs and seasoning well together. Shape into cakes on a wet board.

2 Dip into flour, egg and dried crumbs. Fry in hot fat until golden. Drain on kitchen paper and keep warm.

3 Spread the pineapple with a little French mustard, sprinkle with sugar and fry until lightly coloured. Arrange them on a hot dish and place the pork patties on top. Garnish with spring onion (scallion) or chives.

Creamy horseradish sauce goes well with these.

Crêpes Bologna Style

INGREDIENTS

2 prepared pancakes (from your freezer, see p. 89)
15 g/½ oz (1 tablespoon) butter
1 small onion – finely chopped
15 g/½ oz (1 tablespoon) plain flour (all purpose flour)
100 g/4 oz (¼ lb) minced meat (ground meat)
½ clove of garlic – crushed
2 mushrooms – finely chopped
4×15 ml spoons/4 tablespoons (¼ cup) beef stock (beef broth)
1×5 ml spoon/1 teaspoon (1 teaspoon) tomato purée
1×5 ml spoon/1 teaspoon (1 teaspoon) fresh marjoram – chopped OR pinch of dried marjoram
salt and freshly ground black pepper
2×15 ml spoons/2 tablespoons (2 tablespoons) grated Parmesan or Cheddar cheese
few flakes of butter

METHOD

Cooking time: 25 minutes

1 Put the pancakes on a lightly greased plate. Cover with foil and place over simmering water to re-heat.

2 Melt the butter, add onion, cook gently for 5 minutes, stir in minced meat (ground meat) increase heat and colour lightly. Sprinkle on the flour, mix well, then add stock (broth), garlic, mushrooms, purée and marjoram. Blend well together, season, bring to the boil, reduce heat and allow to simmer for 20 minutes.

3 Put half the mixture on each pancake and roll up. Place on lightly greased ovenproof dish. Sprinkle with cheese and put a few flakes of butter on each. Put under a pre-heated grill (broiler) until cheese bubbles.

Risotto Bolognese

It is worth looking for genuine Italian rice when making risotto. It is a thick grained variety which absorbs liquid well and is soft and creamy; however, long grain will give a good result.

INGREDIENTS

25 g/1 oz (2 tablespoons) butter
1 small onion – finely chopped
2 chicken livers – trimmed and sliced
2 mushrooms – finely sliced
150–250 ml/5–8 fl oz (⅔–1 cup) chicken stock (chicken broth)
1×2.5 ml spoon/½ teaspoon (½ teaspoon) tomato purée
½ clove of garlic – crushed
50 g/2 oz (4 tablespoons) Italian or long grain rice
salt and freshly ground black pepper
2×15 ml spoons/2 tablespoons (2 tablespoons) Parmesan cheese – grated

METHOD

Cooking time: 25 minutes

1 Melt half the butter in a small pan and add the onion. Cook for a few minutes then stir in the liver and mushrooms. Cook quickly for a minute or two. Remove from the heat.

2 Add the rice, purée and garlic and cook for a minute. Pour in a little stock (broth), bring to the boil, reduce the heat and allow to simmer until it begins to thicken. Repeat the process until the rice is tender and the liquid absorbed – you may not use all the stock (broth). Remove from the heat, flake the butter over the surface and stir in with a fork. Turn on to a hot serving dish and sprinkle with parsley.

Serve the grated cheese separately.

*Serve Spanish Omelette with
firm, fresh tomatoes.*

Spanish Omelette

There are many versions of the Spanish omelette,
this is just one. Use whatever you have available
. . . leftover vegetables, a rasher or slice of bacon
cut into small pieces, cold cooked poultry . . .
almost anything savoury that needs finishing up.

INGREDIENTS

25 g/1 oz (2 tablespoons) butter
1 small potato – peeled and finely diced
15 g/½ oz (1 tablespoon) onion – finely chopped
*25 g/1 oz (2 tablespoons) sweet red or green pepper –
finely chopped*
*25 g/1 oz (2 tablespoons) cooked green peas OR frozen
peas, which do not need to be pre-cooked (optional)*
salt and freshly ground black pepper
2 eggs

METHOD

Cooking time: about 20 minutes

1   Melt the butter in a frying pan, add the
    potato and onion and cook gently for 3
    minutes. Add the green or red pepper and
    cook slowly until the vegetables are tender.
    Remove pan from heat.

2   Add peas to pan.

3   Beat the eggs and season well with salt and
    pepper.

4   Return the pan to the heat and pour the eggs
    over the vegetables. Cook over moderate heat
    until just set. Serve sprinkled with parsley.

Pork and Apricot Zingara

Pork and Apricot Zingara

A pork chop may be used in place of the rasher if you have an aversion to fat, but remember to add a little oil to the pan when cooking it.
This dish makes a tasty meal served with tender carrots, broad beans and a jacket potato.

INGREDIENTS

1×100 g/4 oz (¼ lb) slice of belly pork (fatty salt pork)
1×200 g/7 oz (7 oz) can of apricot halves
1 small onion – finely chopped
2×5 ml spoons/2 teaspoons (2 teaspoons) wine vinegar
good pinch of ground ginger
salt and freshly ground black pepper
1×2.5 ml spoon/½ teaspoon (½ teaspoon) cornflour (corn starch), slaked with a little cold water

METHOD

1   De-rind the slice of belly pork (fatty salt pork) and fry slowly to a golden brown – no fat is necessary as the slow cooking draws the fat from the pork. Remove from the pan and keep hot.

2   Add the onion to the pan and cook gently until golden.

3   Drain the apricots and reserve the juice. Cut two of the apricot halves into slices and add to the pan. Cook for a minute or two.

4   Pour the vinegar into 3×15 ml spoons/3 tablespoons (3 tablespoons) of the reserved juice and stir in the cornflour (corn starch) and ginger. Season with salt and pepper and add to the pan. Stirring constantly, bring to the boil.

Serve the rasher with the spiced fruit sauce poured over. Garnish with watercress or parsley. The remainder of the apricots and juices are made into Walnut and Apricot Cream, page 74.

Danish Bacon Chop

A thick slice of boneless back rib constitutes a 'bacon chop'. These are particularly suitable for single meals – quickly cooked, with practically no waste. Serve with a green salad.

INGREDIENTS

15 g/½ oz (1 tablespoon) butter
1×100 g/4 oz (¼ lb) Danish bacon chop
2 shallots – finely chopped
50 g/2 oz (4 tablespoons) long grain rice
freshly ground black pepper
1×5 ml spoon/1 teaspoon (1 teaspoon) Worcestershire sauce
150 ml/¼ pint (⅔ cup) tomato juice

METHOD

Cooking time: about 20 minutes

1 Melt the butter. Trim the rind off the chop and brown lightly on each side in the butter. Remove to a plate.

2 Stir the shallots into the butter and cook gently for a minute or two. Add the rice and continue cooking for 2 or 3 minutes.

3 Replace the chop, pour the tomato juice and Worcestershire sauce over, season with the black pepper. Bring the pan to the boil, reduce the heat immediately and allow to simmer until the bacon is tender and the rice has absorbed most of the tomato juice. The dish should be creamy, not dry.

Serve straight from the pan, garnished with chives.

Danish Bacon Chop

Devilled Lambs' Kidneys

INGREDIENTS

3 lambs' kidneys – skinned, cored and cut into slices
25 g/1 oz (2 tablespoons) butter
½ small onion – finely chopped
4×15 ml spoons/4 tablespoons (¼ cup) dry white wine
or good stock (broth)
salt and freshly ground black pepper
pinch of cayenne pepper
1×2.5 ml spoons/½ teaspoon (½ teaspoon) anchovy
essence (anchovy extract)
2×5 ml spoons/2 teaspoons (2 teaspoons)
Worcestershire sauce
4×15 ml spoons/4 tablespoons (¼ cup) double cream
(heavy cream)

METHOD

Cooking time: 15 minutes

1 Melt the butter; when hot add the kidneys and cook gently for 6 minutes. Remove the kidneys and keep hot.

2 Add the onion to the hot butter and fry gently until soft. Pour in the wine or stock (broth), scraping the pan well, and allow to reduce a little.

3 Stir in the cayenne pepper, anchovy essence (anchovy extract), Worcestershire sauce and cream. Check the seasoning. Bring to the boil and pour over the kidneys.

Garnish with potato crisps (potato chips) and watercress. Serve with boiled rice.

Golden Bubble and Squeak

INGREDIENTS

1 large egg
50 g/2 oz (4 tablespoons) cold mashed potato
50 g/2 oz (4 tablespoons) cold cooked cabbage OR
spring greens
1×5 ml spoon/1 teaspoon (1 teaspoon) white wine
vinegar
salt and freshly ground black pepper
a little oil or lard for frying

METHOD

1 Beat the egg thoroughly.

2 Stir the beaten egg into the potato and cabbage, add the vinegar, season to taste and form into a cake.

3 Heat the oil or lard in a shallow pan and fry the cake until golden on both sides.

Sausage Galantine

INGREDIENTS

100 g/4 oz (¼ lb) carrots – cleaned and grated
225 g/8 oz (½ lb) sausage meat (pork or beef)
1×15 ml spoon/ 1 tablespoon (1 tablespoon) fresh
parsley – chopped
2×15 ml spoons/2 tablespoons (2 tablespoons) medium
oatmeal OR *porridge oats*
salt and freshly ground black pepper
100 g/4 oz (¼ lb) frozen peas – cooked
2×15 ml spoons/2 tablespoons (2 tablespoons) pickled
beetroot – chopped
1 small onion – chopped
1×2.5 ml spoon/½ teaspoon (½ teaspoon) chopped fresh
sage OR *pinch of dried sage*
2 eggs – beaten

METHOD

Cooking time: 1½ hours

1 Well grease a mould or small cake tin, put a small quantity of each vegetable into the bottom to create a design. (This is optional, but it looks nice when turned out.)

2 Mix together the remaining ingredients, season and turn into the mould. Cover with greased foil and tie down.

3 Steam for 1½ hours. Turn out carefully if serving hot, otherwise leave in the mould until cold.

Aubergine (Eggplant) Farçie

INGREDIENTS

1 small aubergine (eggplant)
salt and freshly ground black pepper
1×15 ml spoon/1 tablespoon (1 tablespoon) cooking oil
15 g/½ oz (1 tablespoon) butter
1 small onion – finely chopped
1 tomato – skinned, de-seeded and diced
2 anchovy fillets – chopped
small clove of garlic – crushed
1×5 ml spoon/1 teaspoon (1 teaspoon) fresh herbs –
chopped OR pinch of dried herbs
25 g/1 oz (2 tablespoons) Parmesan or Cheddar cheese
– grated
25 g/1 oz (2 tablespoons) soft white breadcrumbs

METHOD

Cooking time: 40 minutes

1   Cut the aubergine (eggplant) in half along its length and cut around the flesh and across it several times. Sprinkle with salt and leave for about 20 minutes.

2   Rinse, drain and dry.

3   Heat the oil in a frying pan and place the aubergine (eggplant) halves, face down, in it. Fry them for about 8 minutes, turning them over once or twice.

4   Lift from the pan and scrape the flesh carefully out of the skins. Chop the flesh coarsely.

5   Melt the butter in a pan, add onion and cook gently until soft. Add the tomato, garlic, anchovy, herbs, aubergine (eggplant) flesh and seasoning. Heat together well.

6   Fill the skins with the mixture. Sprinkle with the crumbs and cheese. Brown well under the grill (broiler).

When using Parmesan cheese, a little oil or melted butter may be trickled over the top to prevent scorching.

To prepare Aubergine Farçie,
Top right: make several cuts across the
flesh of the halved aubergine;
Centre: fry the aubergine in oil for about 8 mins;
and Right: Aubergine Farçie ready to serve,
garnished with lemon.

Sweet and Sour Chicken Breast

Leftover cold chicken is equally suitable for this Chinese style dish.

INGREDIENTS

1×15 ml spoon/1 tablespoon (1 tablespoon) cooking oil
1 chicken breast – boned and cut into strips.
1 slice of canned pineapple
pinch of ground ginger
2×5 ml spoons/2 teaspoons (2 teaspoons) sugar
1 small onion – finely chopped
1×15 ml spoon/1 tablespoon (1 tablespoon)
wine vinegar
1×5 ml spoon/1 teaspoon (1 teaspoon) tomato ketchup
1×5 ml spoon/1 teaspoon (1 teaspoon) soy sauce
1×15 ml spoon/1 tablespoon (1 tablespoon) sherry
175 ml/6 fl oz (¾ cup) pineapple juice
2×5 ml spoons/2 teaspoons (2 teaspoons) cornflour
(cornstarch)
salt and freshly ground black pepper

METHOD

Cooking time: 20 minutes

1 Heat the oil in a pan, add chicken strips and fry gently until just cooked. Remove to a plate.

2 Cut the pineapple slice into small pieces, add to the oil and cook gently together with the finely chopped onion.

3 Mix all the remaining ingredients together, pour into the pan and cook, stirring constantly, until thick.

4 Replace the chicken and heat through. Pour into the serving dish.

Serve very hot with buttered noodles.

Spicy Chicken Roast

INGREDIENTS

15 g/½ oz (1 tablespoon) butter
1 small onion – finely chopped
1 small orange
2×5 ml spoons/2 teaspoons (2 teaspoons)
Worcestershire sauce
1×15 ml spoon/1 tablespoon (1 tablespoon) tomato
sauce
salt and freshly ground black pepper
Cayenne pepper
1 chicken joint

METHOD

Cooking time: 35 minutes
Oven: 200°C 400°F Gas mark 6

1 Melt the butter in a small pan, cook onion for a few minutes, remove from heat.

2 Take a couple of thin strips of orange rind and slice very finely. Grate the remaining rind and squeeze the juice. Add to the onion, together with Worcestershire and tomato sauces. Bring to the boil, remove from heat.

3 Season the chicken joint, place on lightly greased foil, cover with the sauce and close the foil loosely but securely.

4 Bake in pre-heated oven for 25 minutes.

5 Fold back the foil, baste chicken with the sauce, return to the oven and brown.

Serve hot covered with the sauce, accompanied by potato croquettes and broccoli.

Chicken Breast Paprika

INGREDIENTS

1 breast of chicken
3×5 ml spoons/3 teaspoons (3 teaspoons) paprika
25 g/1 oz (2 tablespoons) butter
25 g/1 oz (2 tablespoons) onion – chopped very finely
1×2.5 ml spoon/½ teaspoon (½ teaspoon) tomato purée
2×15 ml spoons/2 tablespoons (2 tablespoons) dry
white wine
2×15 ml spoons/2 tablespoons (2 tablespoons) double
cream (heavy cream) OR *plain yoghurt*
salt and freshly ground black pepper

Chicken Breast Paprika

METHOD

1   Coat the chicken breast in paprika. Heat the butter in a shallow pan and cook gently on one side for 5 minutes. Turn over and cook the other side for 5 minutes. Lift out of the pan and place in a serving dish. Keep warm.

2   Add the chopped onion to the pan and cook gently until golden. Sprinkle in the remaining paprika, add the white wine, bring to the boil and allow to reduce to half. Stir in the tomato purée and cream, season to taste and pour over the chicken. Serve with freshly boiled rice.

Pigeon with Grapes

The flesh of a pigeon is mainly on the breast; an average sized bird makes a perfect meal for one. If you have the liver, slice it and add to the pan five minutes before the end of cooking time.

INGREDIENTS

1 plump pigeon – trussed
25 g/1 oz (2 tablespoons) butter
salt and freshly ground black pepper
1 small onion – finely chopped
102 ml/4 fl oz (½ cup) dry white wine
1×15 ml spoon/1 tablespoon (1 tablespoon) fresh parsley – finely chopped
1×5 ml spoon/1 teaspoon (1 teaspoon) fresh tarragon – finely chopped OR pinch of dried tarragon
50 g/2 oz (4 tablespoons) green grapes – halved and pipped

To garnish:
2 small triangles of fried bread
a few browned flaked almonds

METHOD

Cooking time: about 1 hour

1 Singe the bird if necessary. Wipe the inside with a damp cloth and sprinkle with salt and pepper.

2 Melt the butter in a sauté pan. When hot, put in the pigeon and lightly brown it on all sides. Season with salt and pepper, add the onion and wine. Reduce the heat, cover the pan and allow to simmer for 30 minutes. Remove from the heat.

3 Tip the herbs and grapes into the pan and allow to simmer, covered, for another 30 minutes, or until the pigeon is tender.

4 Remove the bird on to a hot serving dish. Reduce the sauce if necessary, over a high heat, check the seasoning then pour over the pigeon.

Serve garnished with the fried bread and almonds.

Turkey Wing Divan

Cooked, cold leftover turkey or chicken can be used in place of fresh wing, but reduce the cooking time to 20 minutes.

INGREDIENTS

25 g/1 oz (2 tablespoons) butter
salt and freshly ground black pepper
1 turkey wing
100 g/4 oz (¼ lb) broccoli spears – cooked and drained
1×200 g/7 oz (7 oz) can of condensed cream of chicken soup
2×15 ml spoons/2 tablespoons (2 tablespoons) mayonnaise (see page 34)
squeeze of lemon juice
25 g/1 oz (2 tablespoons) soft white breadcrumbs
few flakes of butter

METHOD

Cooking time: 30 minutes
Oven: 180°C 350°F Gas mark 4

1 Melt the butter in a large pan. Season the turkey wing and sauté in the butter until golden brown.

2 Lightly grease an ovenproof dish and arrange the broccoli spears in it. Lay the turkey wing on top.

3 In a small bowl, mix together the soup, mayonnaise and lemon juice. Pour over the turkey. Sprinkle the crumbs over the top and finish with a few flakes of butter.

4 Cook in a pre-heated oven for about 30 minutes, until golden and bubbling.

Serve garnished with watercress. A baked jacket potato completes the dish.

Pigeon with Grapes

Savoury Chicken Fritters

To use the other half packet of Crispy Batter Mix, see page 68 for Special Apple Rings.

INGREDIENTS

½ packet of Crispy Batter Mix
5×15 ml spoons/5 tablespoons (⅓ cup) of cold water
75 g/3 oz (6 tablespoons) cold cooked chicken – diced
50 g/2 oz (4 tablespoons) cooked mixed vegetables
50 g/2 oz (4 tablespoons) cold mashed potatoes
salt and freshly ground black pepper
oil or fat for deep frying

METHOD

Cooking time: about 5 minutes

1   Mix the batter powder with 5×15 ml spoons/5 tablespoons (⅓ cup) of cold water.

2   Combine the chicken, vegetables and potato and season well. Form into 4 flat cakes. Dip into the batter and cook in pre-heated oil or fat until golden brown. Drain well, and arrange on a hot serving dish garnished with lemon.

Serve with salad and a quick tangy sauce made by mixing a little tomato ketchup and prepared horseradish. Sharpen with a dash of wine vinegar and a few drops of Tabasco.

Plaice Splendide

The majority of white fish dishes are interchangeable. Cod, haddock, whiting, etc., are all suitable but if you are using sole, remember to remove the skin first or ask the fishmonger to do it for you.

INGREDIENTS

175 g/6 oz (6 oz) fillet of plaice – skinned
salt and freshly ground black pepper
pinch of paprika
squeeze of lemon juice
1 large orange – cut in half
15 g/½ oz (1 tablespoon) butter
2×15 ml spoons/2 tablespoons (2 tablespoons)
mayonnaise (see page 34)
4 anchovy fillets – halved
1×15 ml spoon/1 tablespoon (1 tablespoon) French
dressing (Italian dressing)

To garnish:
watercress
small orange – peeled and sliced
cucumber
black olive
2 prawns

METHOD

Cooking time: 15 minutes
Oven: 180°C 350°F Gas mark 4

1   Rinse and dry the fish. Sprinkle with salt, pepper, paprika and lemon juice. Roll up.

2   Place the fish in an ovenproof dish, squeeze one half of the orange and pour over the plaice. Flake the butter over the top and cover with buttered paper.

3   Bake in a pre-heated oven for 15–20 minutes. Remove from the oven and leave until cold.

4   Transfer the fillet on to the serving dish.

5   Squeeze the other half of the orange and stir the juice into the mayonnaise. Add the liquid from the fish cooking dish. Season to taste.

6   Mask the fish with the mayonnaise. Slice the anchovy fillets in half and arrange on top.

Garnish the dish with prawns, watercress and orange slices dipped in French dressing (Italian dressing), and serve with sliced cucumber and a black olive.

Baked Avocado Stuffed with Spiced Crab

If the avocado is soft leave the skin on, otherwise peel it. Rub the other half of the avocado with lemon juice, and make Chilled Avocado Cream Soup, page 17, the next day.

INGREDIENTS

½ large avocado
50 g/2 oz (4 tablespoons) crabmeat – fresh or frozen
(defrosted)
15 g/½ oz (1 tablespoon) butter
1 shallot OR slice of onion – finely chopped
1×2.5 ml spoon/½ teaspoon (½ teaspoon) curry paste
15 g/½ oz (1 tablespoon) sultanas
1×15 ml spoon/1 tablespoon (1 tablespoon) double
cream (heavy cream)
salt and freshly ground black pepper
a little oil

METHOD

Cooking time: 25 minutes
Oven: 180°C 350°F Gas mark 4

1   Melt the butter in a small pan, add the shallot or onion and cook gently until soft. Stir in the curry paste, crabmeat and sultanas and mix well together with the cream. Season to taste.

2   Peel the avocado half, scoop out a little of the flesh, dice and add to the crab mixture.

3   Place the avocado in a small greased ovenproof dish. Stuff with the crab mixture and sprinkle with a little oil. Bake in a pre-heated oven for about 20 minutes.

Serve very hot, sprinkled with parsley.

Fish Crisp

INGREDIENTS

15 g/½ oz (1 tablespoon) butter
150 g/ 4 oz (¼ lb) fresh or frozen cod or haddock steak
1×15 ml spoon/1 tablespoon (1 tablespoon) plain flour (all purpose flour)
salt and freshly ground black pepper
2 tomatoes – skinned, de-seeded and sliced, OR *a little tomato ketchup*
15 g/½ oz (1 tablespoon) cornflakes
25 g/1 oz (2 tablespoons) Cheddar cheese – grated

METHOD

Cooking time: 15 to 20 minutes
Oven: 200°C 400°F Gas mark 6

1 Well butter an ovenproof dish.

2 Defrost the fish if necessary, rinse and dry.

3 Season the flour, coat the fish, place in the buttered dish and cover with the tomatoes or ketchup.

4 Crush the cornflakes and mix with the cheese. Spread over the fish. Bake in a pre-heated oven for 15–20 minutes until a light golden colour.

Tuna and Noodle Casserole

INGREDIENTS

1×213 g can/7½ oz can (8 oz) condensed cream of mushroom soup
1×110 g can/3½ oz can (3½ oz) tuna fish – drained
50 g/2 oz (⅔ cup) egg noodles – cooked and drained
100 g/4 oz (¼ lb) fresh or frozen broccoli – chopped (if frozen – thawed and drained)
salt and freshly ground black pepper

METHOD

Cooking time: 20 minutes
Oven: 180°C 350°F Gas mark 4

1 Mix all the ingredients together and season carefully.

2 Pour into a small greased casserole, cover and bake in a pre-heated oven for 20 minutes, or until bubbling.

Prawn Pasta

Pasta comes in many shapes. I like the shells – particularly cooked, cooled and dressed in salads.

INGREDIENTS

50 g/2 oz (4 tablespoons) pasta shells, cooked and drained
half packet of parsley sauce mix
2 mushrooms (optional)
50 g/2 oz (4 tablespoons) peeled prawns (fresh, frozen or tinned)
25 g/1 oz (2 tablespoons) Cheddar cheese – grated
salt and freshly ground black pepper

METHOD

Cooking time: about 7 minutes

1 Put the pasta shells into a small saucepan.

2 Make up the half packet of sauce mix according to instructions and pour over the shells.

3 If using mushrooms, wipe with a cloth and slice finely. Add to the pan.

4 Stir in the prawns, mix together well. Season and pour into an ovenproof dish.

5 Sprinkle with cheese and grill (broil) until golden and bubbling.

Smoked Fish Special

With some thin tender pancakes a very wide range of dishes can be made – sweet or savoury, economical or frankly luxurious. Cooking for one can so often leave you with tiresome odds and ends. These can be chopped, incorporated into a suitable sauce, seasoned well and used as stuffings. Here are a few ideas, as you look around your larder and store cupboard doubtless others will occur to you.

INGREDIENTS

100 g/4 oz (¼ lb) smoked haddock – cooked and flaked
2×15 ml spoons/2 tablespoons (2 tablespoons) double cream (heavy cream)
squeeze of lemon juice
salt and freshly ground black pepper
25 g/1 oz (2 tablespoons) mature Cheddar OR Parmesan cheese – grated
2 pancakes (see page 89)

METHOD

Cooking time: 20 minutes
Oven: 180°C 350°F Gas mark 4

1 Mix together the fish, cream, lemon juice, cheese and seasoning.

2 Place half the mixture into each pancake and roll up. Place on a lightly greased ovenproof dish and cover with foil. Place in a pre-heated oven until thoroughly hot.

Serve with sauce of your choice. Try adding sliced mushrooms to half a can of condensed mushroom soup. The remainder can be used the following day.

Smoked Fish Special with mushroom sauce.

Dijon Herring

INGREDIENTS

2 small OR *1 large fresh herring*
seasoned plain flour (all purpose flour)
25 g/1 oz (2 tablespoons) butter
1 onion – peeled and very finely chopped
3×15 ml spoons/3 tablespoons (3 tablespoons) cold water
1×15 ml spoon/1 tablespoon (1 tablespoon) wine vinegar
salt and freshly ground black pepper
2×5 ml spoons/2 teaspoons (2 teaspoons) Dijon mustard

METHOD

Cooking time: 15 minutes

1 Cut off the herring heads, clean the fish and retain the roe if any. Dry the fish and tuck the roe inside. Roll in seasoned flour.

2 Melt half the butter in a frying pan and cook the herrings until golden. Remove to a hot serving dish and keep warm.

3 Wipe out the pan, melt the remaining butter and tip in the onion. Cook slowly to a golden brown, stir in the water and vinegar, season to taste. Leave to cook and reduce for a few minutes. When the liquid has almost been absorbed, mix in the mustard. Pour over the herrings.

Serve garnished with crisps (potato chips) and parsley. Tomato and watercress salad offsets the richness of the fish.

Salmon and Anchovy Fish Cakes

Canned salmon makes excellent fish cakes. Make up the whole quantity and freeze half.

INGREDIENTS

1×65 g packet/1×2½ oz (5 tablespoons) instant mashed potato powder – made up and cooled
25 g/1 oz (2 tablespoons) butter
25 g/1 oz (2 tablespoons) plain flour (all purpose flour)
150 ml/¼ pint (⅔ cup) milk
1×225 g can/8 oz (8 oz) can of salmon – drained
2×15 ml spoons/2 tablespoons (2 tablespoons) fresh parsley – chopped
3×5 ml spoons/3 teaspoons (3 teaspoons) anchovy essence (anchovy extract)
freshly ground black pepper
1 egg – beaten
75 g/3 oz (6 tablespoons) soft white breadcrumbs
fat or oil for shallow frying

METHOD

Cooking time: about 20 minutes

1 Melt the butter, add the flour and cook for 2 minutes. Gradually stir in the milk, bring to the boil and cook for a minute or two.

2 Flake the fish into a bowl removing the bones. Combine with the potato, sauce, parsley, anchovy essence (anchovy extract) and pepper to taste. Cover and leave in the refrigerator until cold.

3 Divide the mixture into eight equal sized pieces and shape into cakes, using a little flour.

4 Dip the cakes into first the beaten egg and then the breadcrumbs, pressing them on well with the back of a knife.

5 Heat the fat or oil and fry the cakes until golden on each side. Drain on crumpled kitchen paper.

Fish Quickie

INGREDIENTS

1×75 g/6 oz (6 oz) fillet of white fish (whiting, cod, haddock, etc.)
salt and freshly ground black pepper
2×5 ml spoons/2 teaspoons (2 teaspoons) tarragon vinegar
1×275 g can/10 oz (10 oz) can condensed tomato soup
1 small bag potato crisps (potato chips)
25 g/1 oz (2 tablespoons) Cheddar cheese – grated

Fish Quickie, a crunchy golden supper dish.

METHOD

Cooking time: about 20 minutes
Oven: 190°C 375°F Gas mark 5

1   Rinse and dry the fish.

2   Grease a shallow ovenproof dish and lay the fish in it. Season with salt and freshly ground black pepper.

3   Divide the tomato soup in half. Refrigerate one half for future use. Mix the vinegar into the other portion and pour over the fish.

4   Crush the potato crisps (chips) and mix with the grated cheese. Sprinkle in a thick layer over the fish.

5   Bake in a pre-heated moderate oven for 20 minutes until golden and bubbling.

Chocolate Rum Pot

If you do not like the flavour of rum, add a little of the grated rind of an orange instead.

INGREDIENTS

1 egg – separated
1×15 ml spoon/1 tablespoon (1 tablespoon) castor sugar (granulated sugar)
25 g/1 oz (2 tablespoons) plain dessert chocolate (semi-sweet chocolate) – melted and cooled
2×5 ml spoons/2 teaspoons (2 teaspoons) hot water
1×2.5 ml spoon/½ teaspoon (½ teaspoon) rum or a few drops rum essence

To garnish:
crystallized (candied) violet and angelica

METHOD

1   In a small bowl – beat the egg white until foamy. Add half the sugar and beat again until very stiff and glossy.

2   In a separate small bowl beat the egg yolk and remaining sugar until thick and lemon coloured. Beat in the chocolate, water and rum or essence. Gently fold the egg white mixture into the chocolate. Pour into a small glass dish or chocolate pot. Chill, then garnish.

Chocolate Rum Pot decorated with crystallized violets, angelica and whipped cream.

Crêpes Sicilienne

Chocolate sauce comes ready made in tubes and is a useful addition to the store cupboard.

INGREDIENTS

2 cold pancakes (see page 89)
1 orange – peeled, segmented and cleared of pith and skin
2×15 ml spoons/2 tablespoons (2 tablespoons) orange marmalade
3×15 ml spoons/3 tablespoons (3 tablespoons) chocolate sauce

METHOD

Cooking time: 20 minutes

1   Mix together the orange segments and marmalade. Divide equally between the two pancakes. Fold them up to completely enclose the filling.

2   Place them on a lightly greased plate and cover with greased foil. Place over a pan of simmering water for 20 minutes (or they can be re-heated in a moderate oven if it is in use).

Serve with hot chocolate sauce poured over the crêpes. A light sifting of icing sugar (confectioners' sugar) looks attractive.

Coffee Mallow

INGREDIENTS

6 marshmallows
5×15 ml/5 tablespoons (5 tablespoons) strong hot black coffee
2×15 ml/2 tablespoons (2 tablespoons) double cream (heavy cream)

To garnish:
a few toasted flaked almonds

METHOD

1   Put the marshmallows into a bowl and pour hot coffee over them. Stir well until the marshmallows practically disappear.

2   Leave to cool. Whip the cream and stir into the mixture.

3   Pour into a small glass dish and chill thoroughly.

Serve sprinkled with the flaked almonds and accompanied by a sponge finger.

Banana Cream

INGREDIENTS

1 medium size banana
1×15 ml spoon/1 tablespoon (1 tablespoon) double cream (heavy cream) – whipped
2 cubes from a lemon jelly
3×15 ml spoons/3 tablespoons (3 tablespoons) water

METHOD

1   Dissolve the jelly in the water over a gentle heat. Allow to cool a little.

2   Mash the banana and stir into the jelly. Leave to cool a little more.

3   Stir in threequarters of the cream and pour into a small dish. Leave to set.

4   Spoon or pipe the remaining cream on top. Garnish with chocolate curls and serve chilled.

Grilled Fruit Slices

INGREDIENTS

1 banana – halved
1 slice wholewheat bread – crust removed
3×15 ml spoons/3 tablespoons (3 tablespoons) fruit
juice (i.e. orange, cider or from canned fruit)
25 g/1 oz (2 tablespoons) butter
1×15 ml spoon/1 tablespoon (1 tablespoon) demerara
sugar (light brown sugar)

METHOD

1 Dip the slice of bread in the fruit juice. Melt the butter and fry the bread. Cut into 2 pieces.

2 Cover with the banana and sprinkle with the sugar. Grill (broil) until the sugar bubbles and begins to caramelize. Serve very hot with chilled cream.

Grilled Fruit Slices

Pear and Raisin Crisp

INGREDIENTS

1 pear – cored, peeled, and thinly sliced
1×15 ml spoon/1 tablespoon (1 tablespoon) raisins
1×15 ml spoon/1 tablespoon (1 tablespoon) soft brown sugar (light brown sugar)
1×5 ml spoon/1 teaspoon (1 teaspoon) plain flour (all purpose flour)
pinch of ground cinnamon
1×5 ml spoon/1 teaspoon (1 teaspoon) lemon juice
2×15 ml spoons/2 tablespoons (2 tablespoons) fruit and nut breakfast cereal
15 g/½ oz (1 tablespoon) butter

METHOD

Oven: 190°C 375°F Gas mark 5

1   In a bowl, mix together the pear, raisins, sugar, flour, cinnamon and lemon juice. Turn into a deep greased, ovenproof dish. Sprinkle the cereal over the fruit, flake the butter on top and bake in a pre-heated oven for 25–30 minutes. Serve warm with whipped cream.

Moroccan Orange

INGREDIENTS

1 large orange
1×15 ml spoon/1 tablespoon (1 tablespoon) orange flower water
1×15 ml spoon/1 tablespoon (1 tablespoon) icing sugar (confectioners' sugar) – sifted
1×2.5 ml spoon/½ teaspoon (½ teaspoon) ground cinnamon

METHOD

1   Remove 2 or 3 thin strips of orange peel and slice into fine shreds. Put into cold water, bring to the boil, remove, strain and refresh under cold water. Drain well.

2   Carefully peel the orange, taking care to remove every bit of pith. Slice the fruit thinly, removing pips if any. Arrange on a glass dish and sprinkle with flower water. Chill.

Just before serving, sift the sugar and cinnamon over the orange and scatter the rind on top.

Special Apple Rings

INGREDIENTS

½ packet Crispy Batter Mix
1 small cooking apple
juice of ½ a lemon
2×15 ml spoons/2 tablespoons (2 tablespoons) apricot jam
40 g/1½ oz (3 tablespoons) plain cake or biscuit crumbs
oil or fat for deep frying
castor sugar (granulated sugar)

METHOD

1   Mix the batter powder with 5×15 ml spoons/5 tablespoons (⅓ cup) of cold water.

2   Core and peel the apple and slice into 1 cm/½ inch rings. Dip in the lemon juice.

3   Warm the jam in a small pan until runny, adding a little water if necessary. Dip the rings in jam and then into the cake crumbs.

4   Dip the rings in batter, allow surplus to drain off. Cook in pre-heated oil or fat (190°C 375°F) until golden and apple is tender. Drain well. Toss in castor sugar (granulated sugar) and serve hot.

Honey Shells

Make a batch of these now and again. Just before serving fill them with ice cream, sliced fresh fruit folded into sweetened whipped cream or any mousse of your choice.

INGREDIENTS

75 g/3 oz (6 tablespoons) plain flour (all purpose flour)
pinch of salt
50 g/2 oz (4 tablespoons) castor sugar (granulated sugar)
2 × 15 ml spoons/2 tablespoons (2 tablespoons) clear honey
40 g/1½ oz (3 tablespoons) butter
few drops vanilla essence (vanilla extract)

METHOD

Cooking time: 5–8 minutes
Oven: 190°C 375°F Gas mark 5

1 Sift the flour and salt. Add the castor sugar (granulated sugar).

2 In a small pan, heat the honey to near boiling point, add the butter and vanilla essence (vanilla extract). Stir until melted and tip into the dry ingredients. Mix well to form a batter.

3 Well-grease a large baking sheet and using a 15 ml spoon/ tablespoon (tablespoon), drop the batter 10 cm/4 inches apart. The thin mixture will spread.

4 Bake in a pre-heated oven until light golden, cool slightly and remove with a spatula. Shape over a small lightly greased orange, allow to harden and remove to a wire tray. (If they become too brittle to shape, return to the oven for a minute or two to soften.) These can be stored in an airtight tin.

Fruit and Cream Brulée

Any fruit, suitably prepared, can be used to make this simple sweet. The grill (broiler) must be red hot before you slide the dish under it, the object being to melt the sugar layer and form a thin insulation of caramel before the cream filling spoils by heating.

INGREDIENTS

3 × 15 ml spoons/3 tablespoons (3 tablespoons) double cream (heavy cream)
1 × 5 ml spoon/1 teaspoon (1 teaspoon) icing sugar (confectioners' sugar)
75 g/3 oz (6 tablespoons) fresh, canned or frozen fruit
castor sugar (granulated sugar)

METHOD

Cooking time: about 5 minutes

1 In a bowl, whip the cream until it begins to thicken. Sift in the icing sugar (confectioners' sugar) and whip again until stiff.

2 Prepare the fruit if necessary (i.e. peeling, coring, slicing, etc.). If using canned fruit, drain well. If frozen, defrost and drain. Fold the fruit into the cream. Put into an individual flame-proof dish and smooth the top. Chill well.

3 Sift an even layer 5 mm/¼ inch thick of castor sugar (granulated sugar) over the cream.

4 Place the chilled pudding under the pre-heated grill (broiler) and leave until there is a thin clear layer of golden caramel. Remove at once.

Serve cold.

Grapefruit Mintie

This is a dual purpose recipe. When you want this for a starter use 2×5 ml spoons/2 teaspoons (2 teaspoons) of Crème de Menthe. When preparing it as a pudding use the quantity given below. It is particularly suitable after a rich meal, the liqueur being a 'digestif'.

INGREDIENTS

½ a grapefruit
2×15 ml spoons/2 tablespoons (2 tablespoons) Crème de Menthe

METHOD

1   Remove all skin, pith and membrane from the grapefruit flesh.

2   Arrange in a glass goblet and pour over the Crème de Menthe. Chill well.

Grapefruit Mintie

Honey Snowball

INGREDIENTS

1 large cooking apple
1 sweet biscuit – crumbled
honey
1 × 2.5 ml spoon/½ teaspoon (½ teaspoon) butter
1 small egg white
40 g/1½ oz (3 tablespoons) castor sugar (granulated sugar)

METHOD

Cooking time: 40 minutes
Oven: 180°C 350°F Gas mark 4

1   Wash, dry and core the apple. Slit the skin around the middle.

2   Mix the crumbled biscuit with a little honey and stuff the hollow core. Place the apple in a small greased ovenproof dish and flake the butter over the filling. Pour a little cold water, or cider if you have it, round the fruit, adding a little more honey. Bake in a pre-heated oven until just tender.

3   Whip the egg white until stiff but not dry. Add half the sugar and whip again until very stiff and shiny. Fold the remaining sugar into the meringue, spreading it evenly over the top and sides of the apple. Arrange the cherry and angelica on the top and return to the oven to crisp the meringue.

Serve hot or cold with the syrup from the cooking dish.

Honey Snowball

Omelette Soufflé

This is so simple, looks spectacular and is delicious. Use whatever jam you have, or soft fruit tossed in sugar. A little rum added to the yolks makes it special.

INGREDIENTS

2 eggs – separated
15 g/½ oz (1 tablespoon) butter
salt
3×15 ml spoons/3 tablespoons (3 tablespoons) good strawberry jam
icing sugar (confectioners' sugar) – sifted

METHOD

Cooking time: 6 to 8 minutes

1   In a small bowl, beat the yolks until thick and creamy.

2   Put the whites in a large bowl and add a few grains of salt.

3   Light the grill (broiler).

4   Place the jam in a small pan and put over a very gentle heat to warm through.

5   Whip the whites until stiff, but not dry. Pour the yolks over the whites, and fold in gently but thoroughly.

6   Melt the butter in an omelette or frying pan. When foaming pour in the egg mixture. Cook over gentle heat until well risen and golden brown underneath. Place under the grill (broiler) to colour the top.

7   Transfer to a hot plate, make a shallow cut in the top of the omelette and pour in the hot jam. Fold over and sift the top with icing sugar (confectioners' sugar).

Walnut and Apricot Cream

INGREDIENTS

Canned fruit will last 2–3 days in the refrigerator. Use the other half of the can of apricots for Pork and Apricot Zingara, page 50.

½ can of apricots and juice
1×5 ml spoon/1 teaspoon (1 teaspoon) powdered gelatine
grated rind and juice of ½ a small lemon
2×15 ml spoons/2 tablespoons (2 tablespoons) double cream (heavy cream)
4 walnut halves – chopped

METHOD

Cooking time: 3 minutes

1   Put apricot juice and gelatine in a small pan and heat gently to dissolve.

2   Slice the apricots. Reserve 1 slice of apricot, put the remainder, plus the juice, into the liquidizer and purée, or rub through a sieve. Stir in the rind, and juice of the lemon together with 1×15 ml spoon/1 tablespoon (1 tablespoon) of cream. Mix all well together.

3   Pour into a glass dish and allow to set.

4   Whip the remaining spoonful of cream until thick. Pile on to the dish.

Sprinkle with walnuts and serve chilled.

A Little Apple Pudding

Omelette Soufflé

INGREDIENTS

1 trifle sponge
1 small cooking apple – peeled, cored and sliced
1×15 ml spoon/1 tablespoon (1 tablespoon) soft brown sugar (light brown sugar)
1×15 ml spoon/1 tablespoon (1 tablespoon) water
150 ml/¼ pint (⅔ cup) milk
2×5 ml spoons/2 teaspoons (2 teaspoons) castor sugar (granulated sugar)
1 egg – beaten

METHOD

Cooking time: 20 minutes
Oven: 170°C 325°F Gas mark 3

1 Dice the sponge cake and place in the bottom of a small ovenproof dish.

2 Cook the apple with the brown sugar and water until soft. Mash to a purée and pour over the sponge.

3 Heat the milk with the castor sugar (granulated sugar), pour on to the egg, whisk well together and strain over the apple.

4 Bake in a pre-heated oven until set.

Serve hot or cold, sprinkled with a little icing sugar (confectioners' sugar). This pudding is particularly delicious when just warm.

Orange Frost

Never throw away the skins of citrus fruits. The simplest way to keep them is to grate the rinds, and mix with a little castor sugar (granulated sugar). Put into small jars and store covered in the refrigerator. You have instant natural flavouring for cakes, puddings and sauces. When lemons are scarce and expensive, smear a thin layer of oil over them and store in a cool place. This way they will keep for months. Incidentally, a citrus fruit will yield more juice if warmed slightly before squeezing.

INGREDIENTS

2 small oranges
1 small egg
pinch of salt
2×5 ml spoon/2 teaspoons (2 teaspoons) lemon juice
2×5 ml spoons/2 teaspoons (2 teaspoons) sugar
7 g/¼ oz (1 teaspoon) powdered gelatine
1×15 ml spoon/1 tablespoon (1 tablespoon) water

METHOD

1 Cut one orange in half and squeeze out the juice carefully – do not break the skin. Make the juice up to 150 ml/¼ pint (⅔ cup) with water. Remove any membrane and pith from the skins, then snip a zigzag pattern around the edge.

2 Separate the egg. Add the yolk, salt, lemon juice and sugar to the orange juice and whisk well together.

3 Pour the water into a small bowl and sprinkle on the gelatine. Leave for a few minutes to swell then stir over a pan of hot water until dissolved. Stir into the orange mixture and leave in a cool place until beginning to set.

4 Whip the egg white until stiff, but not dry, then fold into the mixture. Pour into the orange shells and leave in a cool place or refrigerator until set.

5 Peel the second orange and carefully separate the segments. Garnish each orange with the segments.

Lemon Surprise

If the sponge cakes are small, use 2 cakes, or a slice of home-made sponge.

INGREDIENTS

1 trifle sponge cake
3×15 ml spoons/3 tablespoons (3 tablespoons) lemon curd
3×15 ml spoons/3 tablespoons (3 tablespoons) sherry
3×15 ml spoons/3 tablespoons (3 tablespoons) double cream (heavy cream) – whipped

To garnish:
crystallized (candied) rose petal
angelica

METHOD

1 Split the sponge cake into three layers.

2 Take 1×15 ml spoon/1 tablespoon (1 tablespoon) of the lemon curd and stir into the cream.

3 Spread the sponge layers with the remaining curd and re-shape the cake.

4 Sprinkle with the sherry until it is all absorbed.

5 Spread a thin layer of the cream over the cake.

Garnish with rose petal and angelica. Chill before serving.

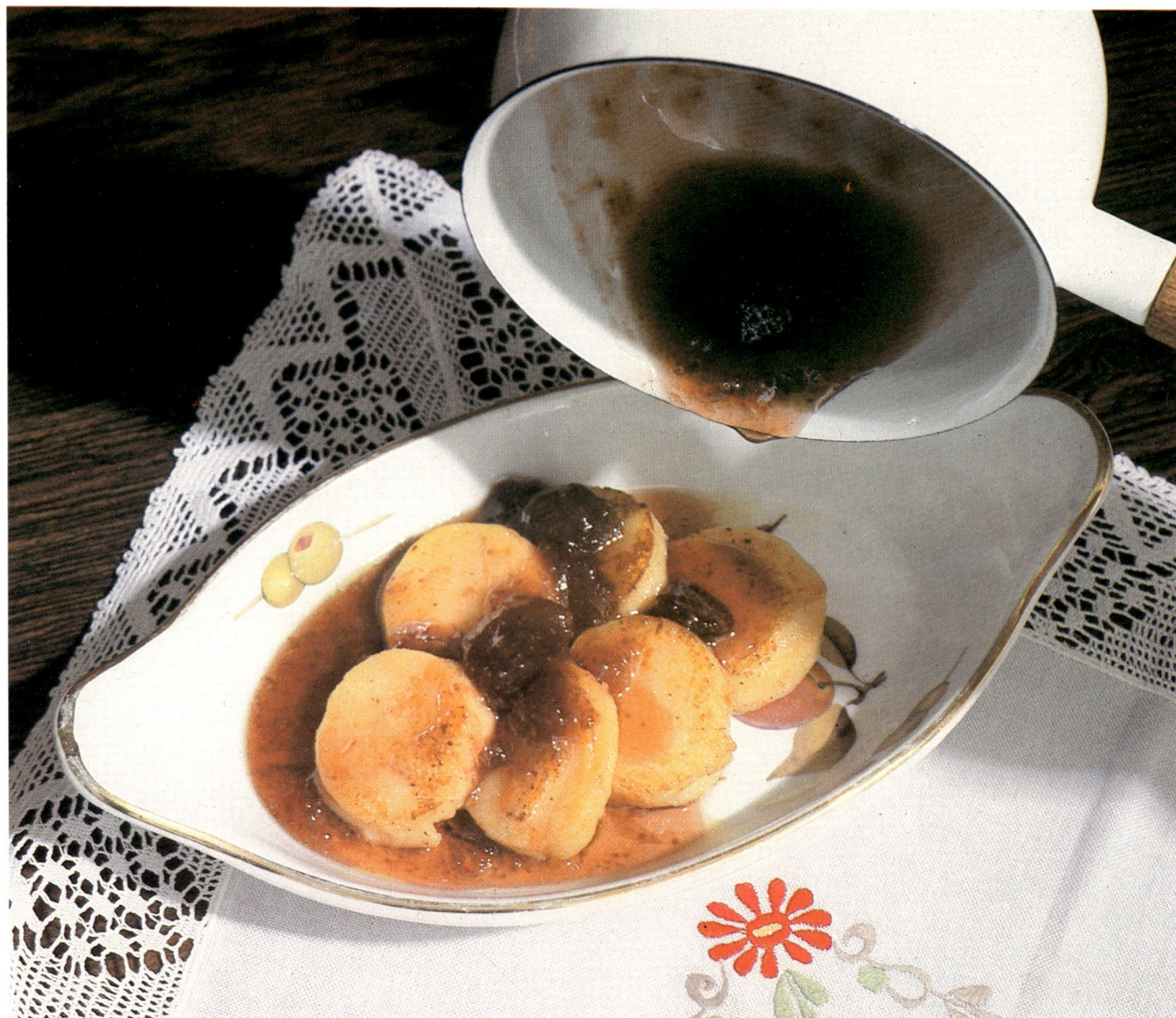

Subrics

Subrics

INGREDIENTS

150 ml/¼ pint (⅔ cup) milk
25 g/1 oz (2 tablespoons) sugar
40 g/1½ oz (3 tablespoons) semolina
1 small egg
25 g/1 oz (2 tablespoons) butter
2×15 ml spoons/2 tablespoons (2 tablespoons) jam – heated
a few drops of vanilla essence (vanilla extract)

METHOD

Cooking time: 15 minutes

1 Bring the milk to the boil in a small pan.

2 Add the sugar and semolina and vanilla essence (vanilla extract) and cook over a gentle heat until thick, then beat in the egg.

3 Pour on to a cold plate and leave until cold.

4 Turn on to a lightly greased board and stamp into rounds using a 5 cm/2 inch cutter.

5 Melt the butter in a shallow pan and fry the Subrics until golden on each side. Serve with hot jam.

Cinnamon and Blackcurrant Pudding

Every now and again I get the craving for a steamed pudding. Here is an unusual, delicious and, alas, fattening treat.

INGREDIENTS

50 g/2 oz (4 tablespoons) plain self-raising flour (all purpose flour+a pinch of baking powder)
pinch of salt
25 g/1 oz (2 tablespoons) butter
2×5 ml spoons/2 teaspoons (2 teaspoons) soft brown sugar (light brown sugar)
1×2.5 ml spoon/½ teaspoon (½ teaspoon) ground cinnamon
1 small egg
2×15 ml spoons/2 tablespoons (2 tablespoons) blackcurrant jam

METHOD

Cooking time: 1 hour

1 Sift the flour and salt into a bowl. Rub in the butter with the fingertips. Add the cinnamon and sugar and mix well.

2 Beat the egg and stir it into the mixture.

3 Lightly grease a small pudding basin and put a little of the blackcurrant jam in the bottom.

4 Pour the pudding mixture into the basin – it should not be more than ⅔ full. Cover with greased foil and tie down.

5 Steam for 1 hour. Just before serving, heat the remaining jam in a small pan. Turn the pudding on to a hot dish and pour the jam over and around it. Chilled whipped cream makes it ambrosial.

Cinnamon and Blackcurrant Pudding

Orange Thins

These are American ice-box cookies. Just slice on to the baking sheet – in 10 minutes they're cooked. Make a batch of dough during a leisure moment and store in the refrigerator. There are many variations – here is one of my favourites. For extra crispness, leave on the baking sheet until cool.

INGREDIENTS

175 g/6 oz (¾ cup) butter
65 g/2½ oz (½ cup) icing sugar (confectioners' sugar) – sifted
100 g/4 oz (1 cup) plain flour (all purpose flour) – sifted
50 g/2 oz (½ cup) cornflour (corn starch) – sifted
3×5 ml spoons/3 teaspoons (3 teaspoons) grated orange rind
vanilla essence (vanilla extract)
castor sugar (granulated sugar) for rolling

Orange Thins

METHOD

Cooking time: 10 minutes
Oven: 190°C 375°F Gas mark 5

1 Beat the butter and sugar together until light and fluffy.

2 Sift the flour and cornflour (corn starch) together, stir into the butter mixture, adding the orange rind and a few drops of vanilla essence (vanilla extract). Wrap the dough in cling film and chill until firm enough to handle.

3 Shape the dough into a roll, about 25 cm/10 inches long on a piece of waxed paper. Roll up tightly and wrap again in foil.

4 When required – grease a baking sheet. Roll the dough in castor sugar (granulated sugar). Cut into 5 mm/¼ inch rounds, place 5 cm/2 inches apart on the sheet. Bake in a pre-heated oven for 10 minutes.

Chocolate Honeys

INGREDIENTS

75 g/3 oz (6 tablespoons) butter
50 g/2 oz (4 tablespoons) honey
15 g/½ oz (1 tablespoon) castor sugar (granulated sugar)
100 g/4 oz (¼ lb) sifted self-raising flour (all purpose flour + 1 level teaspoon baking powder)
25 g/1 oz (2 tablespoons) ground almonds
50 g/2 oz (4 tablespoons) plain (semi-sweet) chocolate
small knob of butter

METHOD

Cooking time: about 25 minutes
Oven: 170°C 325°F Gas mark 3

1 Cream together the butter, honey and sugar. Stir in the flour and ground almonds. Mix well and form into a ball.

2 Grease an 180 mm/7-inch sandwich tin, and press the mixture evenly into it. Mark into portions and prick well.

3 Bake in pre-heated oven. Check after 10 minutes, as it may be necessary to reduce the heat slightly. When you take it from the oven, re-mark the portions. Allow to cool before removing from the tin.

4 Melt the chocolate with 2×5 ml spoons/2 teaspoons (2 teaspoons) of water and the butter.

5 Dip the wide end of the shortbreads into the chocolate and allow to set.

Dropped Scones

These are also sometimes known as Drop Scones, Scotch Pancakes, Flapjacks or Griddle Pancakes.

INGREDIENTS

150 g/4 oz (¼ lb) plain flour (all purpose flour)
1×2.5 ml spoon/½ teaspoon (½ teaspoon) bicarbonate of soda (baking soda)
1×5 ml spoon/1 teaspoon (1 teaspoon) cream of tartare
25 g/1 oz (2 tablespoons) castor sugar (granulated sugar)
pinch of salt
25 g/1 oz (2 tablespoons) butter
1 small egg, beaten
150 ml/¼ pint (⅔ cup) milk

METHOD

Cooking time: 4 to 5 minutes for each batch

1 Sieve the dry ingredients together into a bowl. Rub in the butter, add the egg and enough milk to form a thick batter. (It should just pour off the spoon.)

2 Heat and grease the frying pan.

3 Drop the mixture from the tip of a 15 ml spoon/tablespoon (tablespoon) into small rounds in the pan. Leave plenty of space between. When bubbles appear on the surface, flip over with a palette knife and cook the other side until golden. (It will be necessary to grease the pan after each batch.)

4 Wrap in a clean tea towel to keep warm and moist.

Serve warm with butter and honey.

Macaroons

Make these with that leftover egg white from Olive Chowder, see page 18. They will keep indefinitely in an airtight tin.

INGREDIENTS

175 g/6 oz (6 oz) castor sugar (granulated sugar)
100 g/4 oz (¼ lb) ground almonds
few drops almond essence (almond extract)
1 egg white
few halved blanched almonds
rice paper

METHOD

Cooking time: about 15 minutes
Oven: 170°C 325°F Gas mark 3

1 Line a baking sheet with rice paper (shiny side down). Mix together the sugar, almonds, essence and unbeaten egg white. Mix to a fairly stiff paste. Beat well.

2 Fill the mixture into a piping (pastry) bag, fitted with a plain 5 mm/¼ inch tube, and pipe small blobs on to the rice paper.

3 Press a halved almond on to each one and dust with a little castor sugar. Bake in a pre-heated oven for 15 minutes, or until lightly tinged with gold. Do not over bake. They are nice when slightly gooey inside.

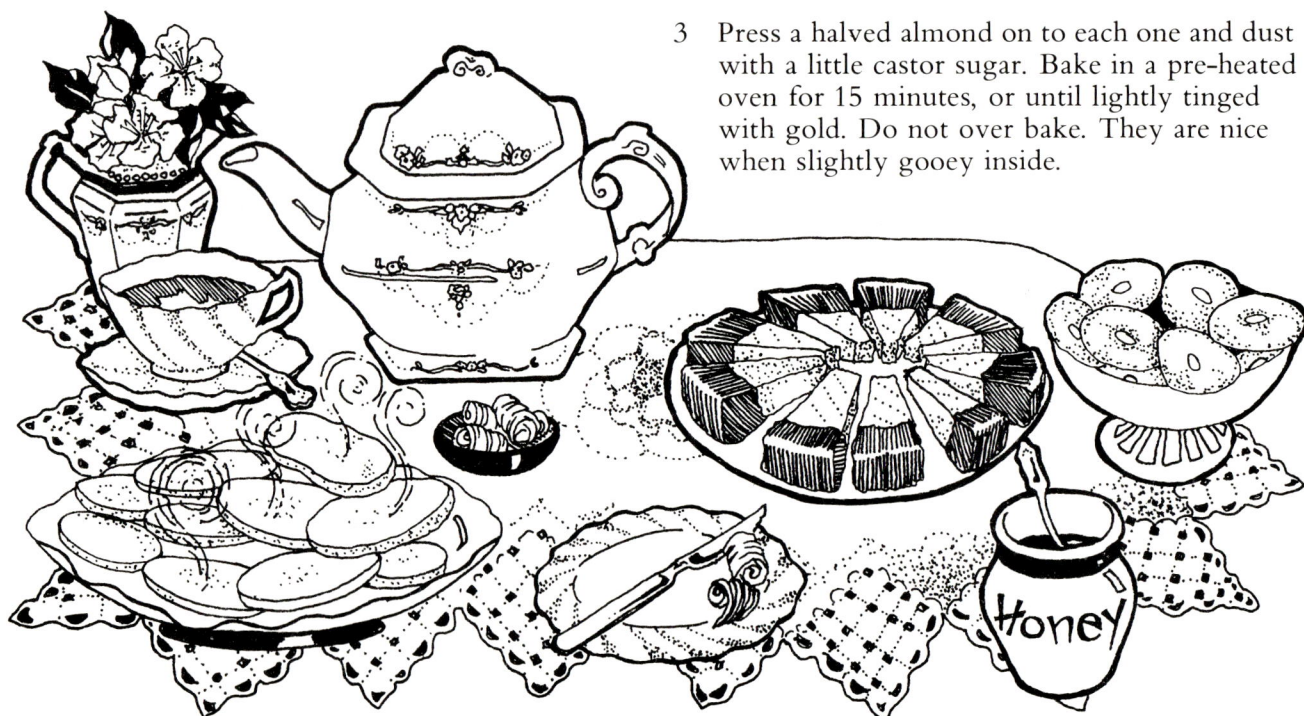

American Brownies

INGREDIENTS

4×15 ml spoons/4 tablespoons (¼ cup) corn oil
50 g/2 oz (2 oz) plain chocolate (semi-sweet chocolate)
175 g/6 oz (6 oz) castor sugar (granulated sugar)
65 g/2½ oz (5 tablespoons) self-raising flour (all purpose flour+½ level teaspoon baking powder)
pinch of salt
2 eggs
1×2.5 ml spoon/½ teaspoon (½ teaspoon) vanilla essence (vanilla extract)
50 g/2 oz (4 tablespoons) walnuts – roughly chopped

METHOD

Cooking time: 30—35 minutes
Oven: 180°C 350°F Gas mark 4

1 Lightly oil and flour a 20.5 cm/8 inch square cake tin. Heat the oil and chocolate in a basin, over hot water, until melted.

2 Sift together the dry ingredients and, off the heat, add all the remaining ingredients to the chocolate mixture. Beat well and turn into the prepared tin. Bake in a pre-heated oven. Leave in the tin to cool, then cut into squares.

Iced Almond Tea

Lemon tea – with a difference. Very refreshing on a hot day.

INGREDIENTS

1 tea bag OR 1×5 ml spoon/1 teaspoon (1 teaspoon) tea leaves
2×5 ml spoons/2 teaspoons (2 teaspoons) sugar
2×5 ml spoons/2 teaspoons (2 teaspoons) lemon juice
250 ml/8 fl oz (1 cup) boiling water
150 ml/4 fl oz (½ cup) cold water
few drops almond essence (almond extract)
ice cubes

METHOD

1 Put tea, sugar and lemon juice in teapot, pour over the boiling water and leave for 10 minutes.

2 Place ice cubes in a glass jug and pour in the cold water and almond essence (almond extract). Strain the tea over the ice. Mix well. Serve in a tall glass garnished with lemon slice.

Tea sometimes becomes cloudy when added to ice, if this happens add a spot of boiling water and it will clear.

Hot Buttered Rum

This will work wonders when you are feeling wretched with a cold, or just as a nightcap once in a while.

INGREDIENTS

1×5 ml spoon/1 teaspoon (1 teaspoon) soft brown sugar (light brown sugar)
boiling water
4×15 ml spoons/4 tablespoons (¼ cup) rum
15 g/½ oz (1 tablespoon) butter
squeeze of lemon juice
nutmeg

METHOD

1 Put the sugar into a mug, cup or *heated* glass. Pour a little boiling water in and stir to dissolve the sugar.

2 Add the rum and butter. Fill up with boiling water and stir in the lemon juice. Grate a little nutmeg over the top.

An Old English Caudle

This is a wonderful 'pick-me-up' if you have a cold or feel slightly tired and weary.

INGREDIENTS

3×5 ml spoons/3 teaspoons (3 teaspoons) fine oatmeal
120 ml/4 fl oz (½ cup) cold water
300 ml/½ pint (1¼ cups) milk
1 egg yolk
1 small wine glass of port or sherry
1×5 ml/1 teaspoon (1 teaspoon) sugar
grated nutmeg or lemon rind to taste

METHOD

1 Put the oatmeal and water into a saucepan, mix together and pour on the milk.

2 Bring to the boil, stirring well. Cook for 5 minutes. Remove from the heat, cool a little and whisk (beat) in the yolk, port or sherry, and sugar.

3 Serve very hot, sprinkled with grated nutmeg or lemon rind.

Normandy Potatoes

Here is an unusual use of instant potato. For variety add a little finely chopped onion, green or red pepper and celery.

INGREDIENTS

1×65 g packet/2½ oz packet (5 tablespoons) instant mashed potato OR 2 medium potatoes – peeled, boiled and mashed
15 g/½ oz (1 tablespoon) butter
1×15 ml spoon/1 tablespoon (1 tablespoon) cider vinegar
salt and freshly ground black pepper
1 dessert apple – peeled, cooked and diced
25 g/1 oz (2 tablespoons) Cheddar cheese – grated
2 slices of bacon
chopped parsley

METHOD

Cooking time: 15 minutes

1 Divide the instant potato powder in two equal parts. Reserve one half for future use. Measure the water for the other half, remove 1×15 ml spoon/1 tablespoon (1 tablespoon) and add the cider vinegar. Make up the instant mashed potato and beat in the butter. (If using fresh mashed potato, add the butter and vinegar at this point).

2 Carefully mix in the diced apple and season to taste.

3 Turn into a small ovenproof dish.

4 Sprinkle the cheese over the potato and place the bacon slices on top.

5 Grill (broil) until cheese melts and bacon curls and crisps. Sprinkle with parsley.

Garlic Tomatoes

These are strictly for garlic lovers!

INGREDIENTS

2 large ripe tomatoes
1×15 ml spoon/1 tablespoon (1 tablespoon) fresh parsley – finely chopped
2 cloves of garlic – very finely chopped
1×15 ml spoon/1 tablespoon (1 tablespoon) olive oil
salt and freshly ground black pepper

METHOD

1 Slice the tomatoes in half horizontally and cut a deep cross on the opened sides.

2 Mix together the parsley, garlic, salt and pepper.

3 Divide the mixture equally between the four halves and press firmly over the tops.

4 Sprinkle with olive oil and grill (broil) slowly until soft.

Chinese Fried Rice

INGREDIENTS

25 g/1 oz (1 tablespoon) butter
4×15 ml spoons/4 tablespoons (¼ cup) leftover cold meat or poultry – finely diced
75 g/3 oz (6 tablespoons) cold cooked rice – well drained
½ small green pepper – de-seeded and finely chopped
1×15 ml spoon/1 tablespoon (1 tablespoon) soy sauce
1 egg – beaten
2 spring onions (scallions) – finely sliced
salt and freshly ground black pepper

METHOD

Cooking time: 15 minutes

1 Melt the butter; when foaming, add the rice and meat, cook over moderate heat, stirring frequently. Add the green pepper and continue cooking for 5 minutes.

2 Sprinkle with the soy sauce, pour in the beaten egg, stir and cook for a further 5 minutes. Stir in the spring onions (scallions), check seasoning. Serve hot, sprinkled with almonds.

Hot Slaw

Try hot slaw for a change. The tight white cabbage is the best for this particular recipe.

INGREDIENTS

½ small white cabbage
1 egg yolk
25 g/1 oz (2 tablespoons) butter
2×15 ml spoons/2 tablespoons (2 tablespoons) wine
OR *cider vinegar*
2×15 ml spoons/2 tablespoons (2 tablespoons) cold water
salt and freshly ground black pepper

METHOD

Cooking time: 15 minutes

1 Wash and shred the cabbage very finely.

2 Beat the yolk with vinegar, water and seasoning. Pour into a saucepan and cook very slowly, stirring constantly until it thickens.

3 Add the cabbage, toss well and continue cooking very gently for about 8 to 10 minutes.

Serve very hot.

Jacket Potato De Luxe

To appreciate the true flavour of a good potato it must be cooked in the skin. Small new ones, scrubbed, cooked and served tossed in melted butter, with chopped fresh herbs; or in the winter, a large baking potato, well scrubbed, baked and served with a topping of your choice such as butter, salt and freshly ground black pepper, crisply fried crumbled bacon, or grated cheese.

INGREDIENTS

1 large baking potato
4×15 ml spoons/4 tablespoons (4 tablespoons) sour cream OR *double cream (heavy cream) soured with a little lemon juice*
salt and freshly ground black pepper
2 shallots OR *spring onions (scallions) if available – finely chopped*
paprika

METHOD

Cooking time: about 1 hour
Oven: 200°C 400°F Gas mark 6

1 Scrub the potato and dry it. If you prefer the skin soft, rub it with a little oil.

2 Bake in a pre-heated oven until tender.

3 Whip the cream until thick, season well and stir in the onions.

4 Remove the potato to a hot dish. Cut a cross in the top. Protect your hands with a cloth and gently press the bottom of the potato to force a little of the inside up through the cross. Top with the sour cream mixture and dust with paprika.

Tasty Leftovers

Most people find themselves with meat or poultry in the refrigerator which wasn't used quite as promptly as intended. My motto is 'when in doubt, throw it out', because you can never be too sure. Yet providing the meat is fresh and you remove it from the wrapping the moment you bring it home and put it in the refrigerator, the following guidelines should be useful.

Certainly, I advise you always to use 'leftovers' as quickly as possible, and once food has been defrosted, never re-freeze it. Make sure that any leftover cooked food is completely cold before storing in the refrigerator.

Uncooked meat	Store for
Beef, veal, pork, lamb	5 days
Steak (frying or stewing)	3 days
Minced meat (ground meat)	no more than 1 day
All offal (including tails, sweetbreads and heart)	1 or 2 days
Pork chops	3 days
Chicken joints	2 days
Chicken – whole	2 days
Pork or beef sausages	3 or 4 days

Magda

Coffee and chocolate go so well together – when I find myself with leftover coffee I make this simple sweet. Use instant coffee if you prefer it.

INGREDIENTS

150 ml/¼ pint (⅔ cup) strong black coffee
1×5 ml spoon/1 teaspoon (1 teaspoon) powdered gelatine
2×5 ml spoons/3 teaspoons (3 teaspoons) powdered drinking chocolate
sugar
vanilla essence (vanilla extract)

METHOD

1   Heat the coffee in a small pan, sprinkle in the gelatine and stir until completely dissolved.

2   Add the chocolate, sugar to taste and vanilla essence (vanilla extract). Leave until cool. Pour into a wine glass and leave to set.

Top with whipped cream and serve with a plain sweet biscuit.

Colcannon

Please do not think of this as just another bubble and squeak; the ingredients are similar, but one has a crisp coat, while this is soft and rich with melted butter.

INGREDIENTS

25 g/1 oz (2 tablespoons) butter or bacon fat
1 small onion – very finely chopped
225 g/8 oz (½ lb) cold boiled or mashed potatoes
100 g/4 oz (¼ lb) cold cooked greens (cabbage, kale or spring greens) – chopped
salt and freshly ground black pepper

METHOD

Cooking time: 10 minutes

1   Melt the fat in a pan, add the onion and cook gently until soft.

2   While the onion is cooking, mash the potatoes until smooth, add the green vegetables, season and beat well together.

3   Combine the onion and potato mixture in a saucepan. Place over heat and stir constantly until thoroughly heated.

Serve in the Irish manner – with a large knob of butter melting over the top.

The Bean Pot

This was a great favourite with my children. It will sit happily in the oven at low temperature for hours. It is a cheap and comforting dish. Leftover poultry, meat or fried sliced sausages can be added to the layers. Experiment with seasoning also. Try a little Worcestershire sauce with cooked crumbled bacon – or curry paste and sweet chutney with cooked sliced chicken. Here is the basic recipe.

INGREDIENTS

1×225 g/8 oz (½ lb) can baked beans in tomato sauce
few drops of vinegar
1 medium size onion – finely sliced
50 g/2 oz (4 tablespoons) Cheddar cheese – grated
1×225 g/8 oz (8 oz) can Italian plum tomatoes, in their juice – sliced
3×15 ml spoons/3 tablespoons (3 tablespoons) soft white breadcrumbs
salt and freshly ground black pepper

METHOD

Cooking time: 25 minutes
Oven: 180°C 350°F Gas mark 4

1 Layer the ingredients into a small deep casserole, seasoning each layer. The top layer being 1×15 ml/1 tablespoon (1 tablespoon) each of breadcrumbs and cheese mixed together.

2 Bake in a pre-heated oven for 25 minutes until golden and bubbling. Garnish with bacon roll and watercress.

Ham and Raisin Balls

A few leftover scraps of boiled bacon are rapidly turned into something special in this simple recipe.

INGREDIENTS

1×15 ml spoon/1 tablespoon (1 tablespoon) seedless raisins – finely chopped
50 g/2 oz (4 tablespoons) cold cooked rice – well drained
75 g/3 oz (6 tablespoons) cold cooked bacon or ham – finely chopped
1×5 ml spoon/1 teaspoon (1 teaspoon) Dijon mustard
2×5 ml spoons/2 teaspoons (2 teaspoons) fresh parsley – chopped
2 eggs
1×5 ml spoon/1 teaspoon (1 teaspoon) plain flour (all purpose flour)
salt and freshly ground black pepper
grated nutmeg
4×15 ml spoons/4 tablespoons (4 tablespoons) soft white breadcrumbs
oil or fat for deep frying

METHOD

Cooking time: 10 minutes

1 In a large bowl mix together the raisins, rice, bacon, mustard, parsley, 1 beaten egg, flour and seasoning.

2 Shape into balls and dip into the second beaten egg and breadcrumbs. Fry in hot, deep fat or oil until golden brown. Drain well.

Serve garnished with fresh tomato. Spinach goes well with these.

Cecil Pasties

If there is a little leftover lamb, make it into these and freeze the surplus. Useful for unexpected guests.

INGREDIENTS

100 g/4 oz (¼ lb) shortcrust pastry
100 g/4 oz (¼ lb) cooked, cold, minced lamb
1 small onion – minced
1×15 ml spoon/1 tablespoon (1 tablespoon) chopped walnuts
salt and freshly ground black pepper
1×5 ml spoon/1 teaspoon (1 teaspoon) lemon rind (lemon zest) – grated
1×15 ml spoon/1 tablespoon (1 tablespoon) melted butter
a little chopped fresh mint
1 egg – beaten

METHOD

Cooking time: 30 minutes
Oven: 220°C 425°F Gas mark 7

1 Mix together the lamb, onion, walnuts, lemon rind, melted butter and mint. Season well.

2 Roll out the pastry on a floured surface and stamp out 10 cm/4 inch rounds.

3 Divide the meat mixture and put in the centre of the pastry. Damp the pastry edges, fold over to form a pasty and press the edge to seal. Crimp with the fingers.

4 Brush with beaten egg and place on a baking sheet. Bake at high temperature for 15 minutes then reduce oven to 190°C 375°F Gas mark 5 for a further 15 minutes.

Serve hot or cold, garnished with lettuce and tomato.

Date Fingers

Every now and again I find myself with yolks or whites of eggs. The whites are no problem; they will keep, covered, in the refrigerator for a couple of weeks. The yolks are more difficult to keep as they tend to 'skin' on top, and I like to use them at once. These fingers freeze well.

INGREDIENTS

100 g/4 oz (¼ lb) soft brown sugar (light brown sugar)
100 g/4 oz (¼ lb) butter
pinch of salt
few drops vanilla essence (vanilla extract)
3 egg yolks
1×15 ml spoon/1 tablespoon (1 tablespoon) cold water
100 g/4 oz (¼ lb) plain flour (all purpose flour) – sifted
225 g/8 oz (½ lb) stoned (pitted) dates – chopped
50 g/2 oz (¼ cup) shelled walnuts – chopped
25 g/1 oz (2 tablespoons) icing sugar (confectioners' sugar) ⎤
1×5 ml spoon/1 teaspoon (1 teaspoon) ground cinnamon ⎦ sifted together

METHOD

Cooking time: 25 minutes
Oven: 180°C 350°F Gas mark 4

1 Cream the sugar and butter well together with salt and vanilla essence (vanilla extract), until light and fluffy.

2 Beat the egg yolks with the water and stir into the creamed mixture.

3 Add the flour, dates and nuts. Stir until well blended.

4 Spread the mixture in a well greased shallow tin 25×18 cm/10×7 inches. Bake in a pre-heated moderate oven for 25 minutes. When cool, make into fingers.

5 Keep the icing sugar (confectioners' sugar) mix in a small covered jar and dust the fingers just before serving.

Chicken in Redcurrant sauce

INGREDIENTS

100 g/4 oz (¼ lb) chicken – cold, cooked and sliced
15 g/½ oz (1 tablespoon) butter
2×15 ml spoons/2 tablespoons (2 tablespoons)
redcurrant jelly
4×15 ml spoons/4 tablespoons (¼ cup) red wine
1×5 ml spoon/1 teaspoon (1 teaspoon) meat extract
1×5ml spoon/1 teaspoon (1 teaspoon) orange rind –
grated
large pinch of grated nutmeg
salt and freshly ground black pepper

METHOD

Cooking time: 20 minutes
Oven: 180°C 350°F Gas mark 4

1 Grease a small ovenproof dish and lay the chicken in it.

2 Combine the remaining ingredients in a small saucepan, and bring to the boil, making sure the jelly has dissolved. Season to taste.

3 Allow to cool and pour over chicken. Cook in a pre-heated oven for 20 minutes.

Basic Pancake Batter

Pancakes are a tasty solution for leftovers. A pancake must be thin to be good. It's worthwhile buying a small pan and keeping it especially for the purpose. It should not need washing – this makes them stick. Just wipe it out with a dry cloth. A little salt will remove any stubborn bits. I find lard is the most satisfactory frying medium. This batter can be mixed in a liquidizer. Make a batch, use some and freeze the remainder, wrapped in twos and threes.

INGREDIENTS

100 g/4 oz (¼ lb) plain flour (all purpose flour)
2 eggs
pinch of salt
300 ml/½ pint (1¼ cups) milk OR milk and water
25 g/1 oz (2 tablespoons) melted butter

METHOD

Cooking time: about 15 minutes

1 Sift the flour and salt into a bowl and make a well in the centre.

2 Break the eggs into the well, add half the liquid and the melted butter and beat well to a smooth batter. Stand aside in a cool place for 10 minutes. When ready to cook, stir in the remaining liquid.

3 Lightly grease the base of a frying pan and when hot pour in a little of the batter; tip and rotate the pan until a thin skin forms, then cook until golden underneath. Turn over and cook the other side.

4 Slide on to a warm plate and cover with a folded tea towel until all the batter is used up.

Freezing

All foods should be cold before wrapping or packing for the freezer.

Exclude as much air as possible before sealing. Flavour and texture are affected if this is not done. Remember that foods expand as they freeze, so always leave space at the top of the container.

Label every item clearly with contents and date. Some people use different coloured labels for meat, vegetables, etc. The majority of foods keep well for 6 months. However, I use up my own frozen foods within 3 months, as I have a theory that long freezing detracts from the quality of the dish.

DEFROSTING

It is difficult to generalize when giving advice about defrosting frozen foods, but these are the guidelines which I follow:
I cook vegetables from frozen. I defrost poultry and meat in the refrigerator, while other frozen foods I defrost at room temperature.

Herbs

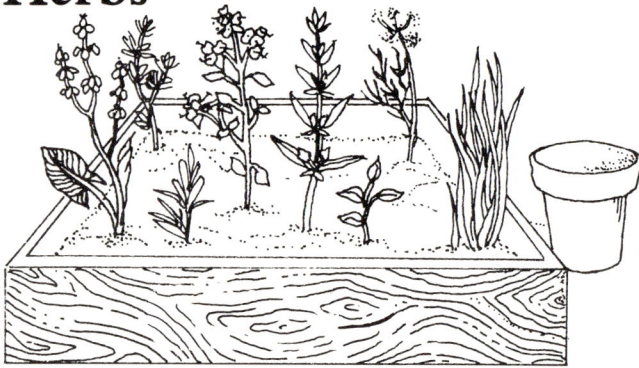

In 1615 Gervase Markham wrote in *The English Housewife* . . . 'The first step to skill in cookery is to have a knowledge of all sorts of herbs belonging into the kitchen, whether they be for the pot, for sallets, for sauces, for servings, or for any other seasoning or adorning, which skill or knowledge of the herbs she must get by her own true labour and experience.'

Herbs are the leaves of aromatic and other plants and vegetables. In many instances the flowers, roots, buds, stems and seeds are also used.

Fresh herbs contain more of the volatile oils that give the flavour and aroma to food, but not unfortunately all year round; the fragrancy can however be retained by drying. If you grow your own herbs, collect them on a dry day, and just before they flower. Dry in the sun or a very low oven. They take between 1 and 1½ hours. Tie in bunches, put in paper bags and hang up in a cool, dry place.

Use all herbs with discretion, because they should enhance not overpower the dish. Here is a list of common herbs and their uses.

Anchusa:	*blue flowers used as garnish for salads*
Angelica:	*stem is crystallized (candied) for cake decoration fruit cups, tisane*
Balm:	*fruit cups, tisane*
Basil:	*tomato and cheese dishes, sauces*
Bay leaves:	*sauces, savoury and sweet dishes*
Bouquet garni:	*consists of chopped, dried thyme, parsley stalks and a bay leaf (or can be whole and fresh)*
Bergamot:	*dried in pot pourri; infusion of fresh leaves makes Oswega Tea*
Caraway:	*seeds for cakes*
Chervil:	*omelettes, salads*
Chives:	*salads, cream cheese, garnish*
Comfrey:	*stews, soup*
Dandelion:	*leaves in salad, flowers as tisane roots are dried and ground to make 'coffee'*
Dill:	*fish, stews, soups*
Elderflowers:	*wine, salads and syrup. Berries also used for wine*
Fennel:	*fish and sauces for fish*
Fines Herbes:	*a collection of chopped, mixed herbs used in classical cookery; parsley, chives, chervil and tarragon*
Garlic:	*salads and dressings, stews, soups*
Horseradish:	*pungent root is grated and mixed with cream, for meat and fish*
Marigold:	*flowers in salads, buds pickled*
Mint:	*sauces, new potatoes, peas and salads*
Onions:	*stews, soups, sauces and salads*
Parsley:	*garnishing, salads, sauces, stuffings*
Pot Marjoram:	*stews, soups and stuffings*
Rosemary:	*lamb, forcemeat and stews*
Saffron:	*rice, bread and cakes*
Sage:	*stuffing, pork, duck and goose*
Sorrel:	*puréed as a vegetable, salad*
Savory:	*stews, sauce for broad beans*
Tarragon:	*sauces, fish, chicken*
Thyme:	*sauces, stuffings, stews and forcemeat*
Violets:	*salads, crystallized (candied) for cake and sweet decoration*

Golden Herb Sauce

There is not always time to make elaborate sauces and simple cooking doesn't call for them. This easy recipe is delicious on vegetables, fish and egg dishes. It turns a fried egg or mashed potato into something special! Please do not economize by substituting margarine. This sauce depends on butter for the excellence of flavour. Use herbs suited to the dish in hand; for example, fennel on fish, sage on a gammon steak.

INGREDIENTS

25 g/1 oz (2 tablespoons) butter
1×15 ml spoon/1 tablespoon (1 tablespoon) wine vinegar
1×15 ml spoon/1 tablespoon (1 tablespoon) fresh herbs; tarragon, chervil, parsley, thyme, lovage, savory and sage – all chopped
salt and freshly ground black pepper

METHOD

1 Melt the butter in a small pan and allow to colour carefully to a light golden brown.

2 Add the vinegar and herbs, season, and pour, whilst still frothing, over the dish.

90

Spices

A varied selection of spices is a boon to any cook as they add their individual flavour and aroma to most sweet or savoury dishes. Made from plant roots, stems, bark, leaves or fruits, spices are imported mainly from the Tropics and Far East. As they generally have a strong flavour only small quantities are needed to enhance the flavour of even plain dishes.

To help you start a spice shelf the list opposite includes the most common spices and their uses, but blends such as curry powder and mixed spice are also very useful.

Storage is all important. To keep flavours intact always keep your spices in an airtight container in a cool, dry place, away from direct sunlight.

Allspice:	*cakes, puddings, soups, meat and vegetables*
Cayenne:	*extremely hot; sauces, soups, cheese dishes, and eggs*
Chilli powder:	*very hot; bean, egg and vegetable dishes, soups*
Cinnamon:	*puddings, mulled wines, cakes, chutney, mincemeat*
Cloves:	*stewed fruits, meat dishes, sauces, for puddings, cooked glazed hams*
Ginger:	*cakes, beer, pickles and chutneys, Chinese cooking, marinades*
Mace and Nutmeg:	*Mace is the lacy covering of the nutmeg and is more pungent than nutmeg; puddings, sauces, cakes, milk drinks, nogs and cream sauces*
Paprika:	*goulash, chicken, sauces, rice, eggs and cheese dishes*
Pepper (black):	*the whole berry; very aromatic and hot; soups, stews, sauces etc.*
Pepper (white):	*the same berry, with outer covering removed; hotter than the black; soups, stews, cream sauces*
Turmeric:	*kedgeree, curry powder, fish soups and stews, eggs and sauces*
Vanilla:	*cream, puddings, cakes, biscuits, sauces*

Banana and Date Chutney

INGREDIENTS

3 large bananas
100 g/4 oz (¼ lb) stoned (pitted) dates – sliced
100 g/4 oz (¼ lb) cooking apples – peeled, cored and sliced
225 g/8 oz (½ lb) small onions – peeled and finely sliced
25 g/1 oz (2 tablespoons) crystallized (candied) ginger – sliced
1×2.5 ml spoon/½ teaspoon (½ teaspoon) ground allspice
1×5 ml spoon/1 teaspoon (1 teaspoon) curry powder
3×5 ml spoons/3 teaspoons (3 teaspoons) salt
120 ml/4 fl oz (½ cup) treacle
150 ml/¼ pint (⅔ cup) vinegar
120 ml/4 fl oz (½ cup) water

METHOD

Cooking time: about 2 hours
Oven: 140°C 275°F Gas mark 1

1 Peel and thickly slice the bananas.

2 Put all the ingredients into a casserole and mix well.

3 Cover and cook in pre-heated oven until dark and thick.

4 Turn into hot jars and seal with plastic screw-tops or tie down squares of cotton dipped in paraffin wax.

INDEX